2--

PSYCHIC PHENOMENA

Revelations
and
Experiences

PSYCHIC PHENOMENA

Revelations
and
Experiences

by Dorothy Bomar Bradley
and
Robert A. Bradley, M. D.

PARKER PUBLISHING COMPANY, INC
West Nyack, New York

Seventh Printing.....October, 1971

PRINTED IN THE UNITED STATES OF AMERICA
B & P

Dedication

To those who have gone before, to those now struggling to be, but more importantly to those yet to come who, holding sacred the integrity of their own minds even in the face of censure from their fellow men, will dare to speak their true thoughts.

Introduction

This book represents the result of many long years of searching for a meaning to our existence in the here and now. Even though these years were filled with many other pursuits, our searching was never forgotten or abandoned. It was like a particularly interesting thread running through a fabric, appearing, disappearing, only to emerge again in another place complementing and enhancing the pattern of our lives.

For my wife and I the search started in earliest childhood in diametrically opposed religions. Yet, interestingly enough, each of us found the attitude of authority over our minds in organized religion to be suffocatingly oppressive. The road we have emerged upon and are travelling in our quest for a deeper meaning to life is one that we sometimes feel we have hewn out of sheer rock. For in determining our course, it has been necessary to rend asunder the sacred shroud of conformity and be daring enough to think for ourselves.

The first real parting of the oppressive clouds came with the discovery that in the outer ring of the family circle was a child who was naturally endowed with intuitive perception. It was through this child that we first became aware of what seemed like the almost miraculous workings of the human mind. And our new awareness opened door after door, after door, each one revealing vistas more awe-inspiring than the one before.

In observing each new splendid view that came into focus, we made every effort to keep a firm footing and a clear head. We tried to find reliable data and make reasonable deductions. Soon came the time when we had to ask ourselves, "If these things are true, and we are forced to believe that they are true simply because they are there, then what can we infer from this is to be the true nature of man, his world and his destiny?"

Seeking these truths for ourselves, we were made ever more aware that the academic parapsychologists tend to ignore the religious and spiritual aspects in their studies of the nature of man. They are so very afraid of destroying the image they have recently been trying to build up as men of science. In their over-zealousness to prove themselves they take the attitude that anything that cannot be repeated at our will is the mere product of a credulous mind or of charlatanism. We, however, feel that theirs is a limited and partial view with no possible hope of explaining the whole.

Ours are not mere personal theories dreamed up without any basis in fact. In the process of our searching we found more than we had ever hoped to find. We found that there is almost no limit to what the human mind is capable of, and, once a finding was made, we always tried to make good use of it. That we were successful is evidenced in the fact that our findings were used in pioneering psychosomatic obstetrics, giving results far beyond what we had even dared hope for. We found our theories to be equally applicable in a beneficial way when used therapeutically in almost every other area of human behavior and endeavor, including parent education, marriage counseling, and psychotherapy. Each area is based upon a format of comprehensive living, including the levels of awareness, the development and utilization in everyday life of interrelationships not only of the mind and body, but also of the soul.

This approach to the overall practice of medicine could appropriately be labeled *psychopneumasomatic* or *comprehensive medicine*. We found that one of the most important tools necessary in achieving these goals is medical hypnosis, which provides an efficient means of studying the subconscious. This, in turn, led to the question, "If problems that have been rejected and submerged in your mind can make you ill, can the disposition of the problems and the proper use of your mind make you well?" And this quite naturally led on to another question, "Are thoughts really things?" So we were led to the whole interesting subject of the instinctual functions of man. Close after came the questions, *"Can the human subconscious function independently of the body and, if so, what happens at bodily death?"*

In our unceasing and ubiquitous searching for fragments of truth, through various doctrines and philosophies, we have come to feel very strongly about the ever-continuing personal identity of man *before birth,* and *after death,* and the resulting restrictions and responsibilities that this entails. We do not pretend to have all the answers; we still trip and fall over the rocks in our path. We still have moments of despair that we shall never puzzle our way out of the mazes we find ourselves in from time to time, but our new-found beliefs in the ultimate goodness of man and ultimate justice give us the courage to stumble on.

Our resolve to keep an open mind and to face squarely the fact that what psychiatrists call effects are really causes, has given us many dark hours. In working our way out of these dark hours we have come upon a philosophy of life that has not only helped us, but, if the increasing demand for our lectures is any indication, many others. So let us recognize and dispose of the opposition by saying that for us it works, and all the resulting sidelights of this search, such as extra-sensory perception, hypnosis and related phenomena of the mind have enriched our lives and filled our days with exciting new discoveries. More importantly, the spiritual values we have found have caused us to rush ahead joyfully in our eagerness to meet our respective destinies. May it so be with you.

The Authors

CONTENTS

PSYCHIC PHENOMENA

Revelations
and
Experiences

Chapter 1

A Strange
Psychic Experience

Arising before anyone else one morning, I (Dr. Bradley) descended the stairs of our big old house, reached for a cigar and strolled into the empty drawing room to use the heavily-weighted lighter that was resting on a marble-topped table. As my hand approached it, I was startled to see the lighter gently rise and float about a foot away, coming silently to rest upon its side.

In bewilderment I examined it minutely; there were no strings attached, all the other occupants of the house were still upstairs sleeping. I noticed that when deliberately tipped over, no matter how slowly it was pushed off balance, the lighter would fall noisily with a metallic clink, not silently.

One often reads of similar, unexplained physical happenings occurring to others and dismisses them with a shrug of skepticism. Surely, one says, these happenings can be traced to hallucinations, practical jokes, trickery, fraud, etc. But let it happen to you, just *once* let it happen to you! It takes only one white crow to prove that all crows aren't black. It may take only one clear-cut thing without a known explanation, happening to you personally, when you are convinced that no fraud or trickery could have been involved, to start you on a train of thought in search of an explanation. Such a train of thought seldom moves out of the station under power of other people's experiences (unreliable!), but let it happen to *you* and, hang on for the ride! What could possibly make it move? What is the source of expended energy involved? Why did it happen to me—or thee?

Such unaccounted for things have happened to our family many times, starting a train of thoughts and a serious search for explanations which continue to enrich our lives in many ways. In sharing our experiences of paranormal phenomena with others, we have found an ever-increasing public interest, for the hypothetical explanations of how and why such things occur overlap and relate in practical ways to each of us in our everyday living. Too, these explanations relate significantly to our inevitable dying.

This book is necessarily written by *two* people and is a combination of two obviously separate styles. We have been man and wife for twenty-seven years and have *together* searched libraries and avidly read; interviewed people with similar experiences; sought out and sat in seances with every "sensitive" or medium available; attended lectures dealing with this subject; participated in study groups; held and led discussion groups with those whose intellect and open-mindedness we respected; and we have in general shared the most rewarding and meaningful "hobby" possible for man and wife. Any attempt by either of us alone to encompass the breadth of this subject would be as ineffectual as trying to perform with one-half of a pair of scissors, for, as you will discover, this trip will take us in many directions; we cannot be confined to a single entity, even if we tried.

The subject involves the very paving material of the road of life, and an awareness of how to apply it adequately will determine whether that road is bumpy or smooth.

The hypothetical explanations of the forces involved in the phenomenon of the floating lighter, previously described, will not only invoke thoughts of material things but will also lead to consideration of spiritual functions.

As a practicing physician I have observed many times the fundamental truth that the wife and mother is the spiritual hub of the family wheel. In dire stress all members turn to the mother for her support. The father compares with the rim of the wheel constantly meeting the outside world. The children compare with the multiple spokes of the wheel, lending their individual support to the structure. From the spiritual standpoint the hub is the most important part, upon which the rest depends; our home is no exception. The rim may get worn and bent, yet still the wheel goes on. An occasional spoke may be lost or weakened, yet the wheel goes on. However, to lose the hub would result in complete collapse of the structure and the loss of function.

Therefore, the spiritual facets of the subject material of this book are primarily dealt with by the hub of our family, Mrs. Bradley, whose keen intuitive depth of insight we have learned to rely upon; whose unerring feminine judgment has so often proved exasperatingly right; and whose faith and strength of character rebuffs the storms of stress like the rock of Gibralter.

Join us. Take a comfortable seat on our train of thought, for the trip will lead down many valleys, up many hills, to many wonderful places. Take in all the scenery, dwell thoughtfully on what you experience. Here is the road we have found to serenity of mind, to effective relationship with others, to facts that back up faith in religious concepts and life after death. Regardless of your present station in life, join us on this train trip. Here we go, from things to thoughts, to theories that just may alter your way of life as it has ours!

Chapter 2

Paranormal
Physical Phenomena

The floating cigarette lighter, although perhaps enough in itself, was not the only phenomenon that started us thinking. Similar phenomena frequently occurred to us. We do not understand why things of this type happen to some people more than to others. It may be that we are simply lucky, or perhaps there is purpose and reason and a plan behind such happenings.

We would like to share some of these experiences with you. They will not all fall into the category of super-investigated irrefutable paranormal or extrasensory phenomena of professional psychic investigators, but they happened to us personally, and we do not have a conventional explanation for them.

The first things that shook us out of our conformist world of pat answers involved our youngest nephew, Mark. When he was at the age of two we left him at a friend's home expecting to be absent for at least two hours at a meeting. I had a sudden change of plans and returned in about twenty minutes to find him completely dressed in his heavy outdoor clothing, snow suit, boots, mittens and cap. I indignantly asked the baby sitter why he had left him in this heavy clothing. He answered that he had no sooner taken off the child's wraps than Mark started to redress himself, insisting all the while "Aunt D. is coming." And when the sitter protested that I wouldn't be back for hours still, the child persisted in having his own way.

As the sitter finished telling me this, little Mark looked up at me and said, "I knews you wuz comin'." In *his* mind there was no doubt.

Many other things of this nature happened to us, one of the most outstanding occurring a few months later during the Christmas holidays. I had just returned from Christmas shopping and was wrapping the gifts I had purchased, secluded in my sitting room with the door closed. Mark rapped on the door and asked if he might watch. I said, "No, because some belong to you. But, if you like, you may watch me tie on the ribbons." When the packages were wrapped except for the ribbons, I called him to come in. As he entered the room he gave a mischievous chuckle and said, "It didn't do you no good. I knows what's in them anyway." I said, "Of course you do!" That challenge triggered him into immediate action and he proceeded to point to each and every package (8 or 9) and name its contents. I was amazed enough at his accurate identification, but when he correctly identified one package as containing a child's purse in the unusual form of an Indian doll, I was mystified and more than a little unnerved.

We spent much time trying to understand what we had just experienced. We knew there was no possible way he could have known what I had purchased and the order in which I had wrapped them.

In our efforts to understand this and related experiences, we soon became frequent explorers in the local library, digging and delving for answers. Our search never ceased.

Then came one earth-shaking Saturday, filled with physical things that defied conventional explanation and left three people pale, weak and, let's face it, "shook!"

During the previous winter months our family had been enlarged by the addition of Siegwalt Palleske, professor of foreign languages at the local university.

We had all barely begun to digest the concept of telepathy when we were suddenly faced with vivid evidence of what to us was a whole new world. It was to make significant changes in our approach to and our way of life. This new evidence falls into the category of poltergeist phenomena, or phenomena that involve kinetic energy acting upon physical objects.

In the afternoon of this particular Saturday, the family, who had all been out on a shopping trip, returned home to find the reception hall in chaos. The upright decorative wrought-iron trellis which was part of a large stone planter had torn loose from its moorings and toppled over. Plants were uprooted, dirt was strewn over the adjacent sofa and surrounding carpet.

No amount of investigation and pondering by all of us brought any satisfactory explanation to mind for this senseless bit of destruction.

Later that evening, after the children were in bed, we three adults had settled ourselves on the large curved sectional sofa in our drawing room to watch a late movie on television.

The only illumination in the room was the light from the television and from the adjacent entry hall. I was sitting next to the stone planter when, suddenly, I became aware of a movement. I turned towards the planter to see a leaf nodding slowly up and down. I thought nothing of this, attributing it to air currents. Then it occurred to me to wonder why just *one* leaf on such a delicate plant could be moving and not the others.

I extended my hand but could feel no air currents at all. I asked the others if they had seen the leaf wave. They had not since it was not in their range of vision.

We shrugged our shoulders, dismissed it from our minds, and continued to watch television.

Shortly thereafter while we were all completely absorbed in the movie, a thunderous bolt of noise brought us all instantly to our feet. After we looked wildly at each other, Sieg started at a run to the back of the house to investigate. We combed the house completely and could find nothing out of order nor any explanation for the sound.

Since it *was* a good movie and there was nothing more to be done, we returned to our story with a lingering sense of uneasiness.

About twenty minutes later, I was completely lost in the plot of the play when my nervous system was suddenly shattered by brilliant, blinding light flooding the darkened room. I sat stunned, thinking I was losing my mind. First, *I only* had seen the peculiar movement of the plant and, now, could it be that I was the only one seeing that the lamps on either side of the fireplace behind the television set had both suddenly, simultaneously and soundlessly turned themselves on? I was almost afraid to look at the others, dreading that they would confirm my fears.

I cautiously peered around to look at them and was immediately reassured that this was no self-hallucination. There sat two grown men, white, numbed, stunned, with glazed popping eyes. If it had not been such a shocking experience, I would have gone into hysterical laughter at their very appearance.

The interesting things to note here are these: First, Bob and Sieg remembered that they had each consciously turned off one lamp, to allow only the restful light in the reception hall to enter the room; the television set was plugged into the same outlet as the lamp on the right, and the television did not manifest any current changes. Second, the lamp on the left was plugged into a separate outlet, yet both lamps lit up simultaneously. Investigation proved that one lamp had lit up on the second position of its three-way switch and the other on the third. Neither the lamps nor bulbs had manifested any electrical defects before this phenomenon, and they have shown none since. Manual operation of the switches produced clearly audible 'clicks' yet the lamps had gone on silently.

The events of that Saturday represent only the beginning of this type of physical phenomenon in our lives. We were soon to move into a large old house that proved to be haunted, our beloved *Bradmar*.

Chapter 3

The Spirits of Bradmar

Bradmar is a beautiful, old English Tudor country home that had stood deserted for many months and had suffered badly from vandalism. In its forty-two years, even while occupied by its former owner, it had been badly neglected and allowed to run down.

On a cold, drizzly early spring afternoon, knowing my love for interesting houses, a realtor friend invited us out to see this fine example of English architecture that had been on the market for some time.

Halfway up the long, wooded lane, I took my first glimpse of the house, and my thoughts moved back in time to medieval England. I saw before me a stately manor house of antique brick surrounded by magnificent old cottonwoods. As we moved along the half mile approach, different portions of the house were intermittently visible in the mist. Leaded glass windows sparkled between the trees. Gables jutted out from the steep blue slate roof topped with many tall chimneys.

It seemed so removed from Denver, Colorado. Without really thinking, "I'll take it!" escaped excitedly from my lips.

Take it we did since the house and grounds seemed to be made to order for the needs of our family. We gave it the name *Bradmar* from the combination of our two names, *Brad-ley—Bomar.*

What helped give us courage to tackle the massive job of ʳoration was the advice and supervision offered by a cousin,

Karl Vogel, an interior designer who had moved to Denver for his health and opened a decorating studio. Since he was alone and the house was so large it was decided that he should move in with us.

One day while Karl was supervising the restoration, a former caretaker dropped by out of curiosity to see what we were doing. He was pleased with our plans to restore rather than alter and, during the course of conversation, asked whether we had heard the story of the split beam in the drawing room. Karl didn't know what he referred to and, on questioning, heard a fascinating tale. For some time before her death, the former lady of the house had told friends, servants and members of the family that when she died, she wanted to lie in state in front of the great fireplace and that on this night she would split one of the two large cross beams. She had specified exactly which one. According to the story, the split occurred, precisely in the way she had predicted. We were to hear this story many times from many different sources in the years to come.

Karl was very skeptical of this type of activity. He had always professed disbelief in anything paranormal. Consequently, he was not at all prepared for the events that took place the night of his first occupancy at Bradmar.

There was so much work to be done on the house that it was still unfinished when school opened in the fall. It became necessary to prove that we occupied the house to the school board in order to enroll our three boys. That all members of the family were there all day long wasn't adequate proof. The children were informed at school that they had to sleep there to prove they lived there!

The children took this as an adventure, and it fell to the different male members of the family to take turns staying with them at night.

The morning after Karl's first turn, his disbelief in things paranormal came to an abrupt end. We all chuckled at the expression on his face, it so resembled ours at the time we were introduced to personal experiences of this nature on that memorable Saturday. Karl demanded to know if any of us had been over to Bradmar during the previous night—we assured him that none of us had.

Mysterious footsteps

Because the floors were being sanded it was necessary that they all camp in one of the upper rooms. Karl stated that after the boys had fallen asleep, he was sitting on the edge of his bed for a last cigarette when in the dead silence of the isolated house he clearly heard the slam of the back door. Since he knew the door was locked he presumed that one of the family had come to check on them. He heard footsteps proceeding through the lower floor of the house. It sounded as if they were made by someone in soft slippers. He could distinguish the change in sounds as someone moved from the wood flooring onto the marble of the hall, then to the wood flooring of the drawing room directly beneath them.

There was a pause. Then the steps proceeded back through the house the way they had come. Finally, he again heard the slamming of the back door. He was puzzled as to why no one had called to him, so he went to the window to see who might be leaving. He remains convinced that no one ever left on the road that is the only entrance or exit from this property.

In about a week it again fell his turn to remain over night, and, as he said, if any disbelief remained after the first occurrence, it was completely dispelled by the second. At about the same hour of the night on the second stay, he once again heard the back door slammed. He again heard the same pattern of footsteps approaching through the house, across the marble floor of the great hall, into the drawing room. As they began to retreat he hurried out onto the balcony above the great hall where the footsteps now seemed to be centered. The area was flooded with moonlight from the windows that reach from floor to ceiling of the two-story hall; there was no one to be seen!

Although he did not actually know "who walks at Bradmar," nevertheless, he called out the name of the deceased former owner and asked, "Is that you?" The footsteps came to a halt. He announced, as only a decorator would, "If you don't like the way I'm restoring this house, now is the time to speak up, because, before long it will be too late!"

There was no answering voice, only a brief pause, (He was later to exclaim, "Thank Heaven there wasn't—I don't know what I would have done if there had been!") then the footsteps resumed their retreat to the back of the house, and again came the sound of the slamming of the back door.

Mysterious electricity

As the restoration work continued we found that it was

necessary to rewire the entire house. The electrician who performed this task has never been quite the same since.

His first introduction to the house was in the early days of the restoration when three family members were working in one of the back bedrooms. I was standing in the center of the room and became aware that a yellow light bulb overhead had lit up. I said, "Who turned on this hideous yellow light?" It was immediately obvious to me that no one had, as no one was near the switch.

I noted that the switch was on the "on" position. As I walked over to flip it off, I called down the hall to the electrician to ask if anything he was doing would account for the light turning on. He said, "No, I'm in the linen closet getting supplies." Then he came down to the room where we were still working, stuck his head in the door and said with exaggerated tolerance, as if he were addressing a child, "Mrs. Bradley, this switch has to be turned on before the light will go on." I said, "Yes I know, Tom, but the switch did go to the 'on' position." He looked at me as if I was not quite safe to be with and walked away; several times during the remainder of the morning he would return to stick his head in the door and say worriedly, "Mrs. Bradley, you know that's not possible." I would always answer, "Yes I know, Tom, but it happened!"

Perhaps this incident served to soften the blow of the next event and prevented him from taking off screaming across the fields.

Tom had just finished completely rewiring the last wing of the house. However, that evening when we brought friends to show them through the house not a light in that particular wing would go on. This was especially frustrating as our union electrician had assured me on leaving that afternoon, "It's all fixed!"

We indignantly called the electrician back on the job, and he spent the remainder of that morning trying to determine the source of the trouble. Throughout this time when I (Mrs. Bradley) would pass him in the halls and on the stairs, I would ask about his progress. He would assure me that he would be finishing at any moment.

Around noon, as the men were breaking for lunch, I was coming through the great hall and I could hear him muttering to himself. I looked up to see him walking down the stairs like a man in a daze, staring straight ahead. He seemed completely unaware of my presence and continued to speak only to himself. I was able to catch the words "I know it isn't possible but I saw it!" "I *know* it isn't possible." "I've never seen it before!" I called to him, "Tom, what is it?" In a strained, hushed voice he told me that he had searched all morning to find the cause of the trouble, from the basement to the attic, and finally, in desperation had pulled the newly connected wires out of the metal conduits and found to his utter amazement that the braided cable which he had carefully fed through the conduit and properly connected the day before had become unbraided, scrambled, and disconnected.

Two days later we faced him with yet another problem. Sieg and I were up in the boys' wing of the house; I was in the back room, Sieg was in the hallway. At this particular time Sieg was up on a ladder sanding some woodwork with an electric hand sander. I was startled to hear a groan and a crash. I rushed out to find Sieg sitting on the floor holding his head. He looked up bewildered and indignantly asked, "Did you hit me?" I answered, "Of course I didn't hit you. Besides I was in the back room!" He was holding his hand up to his head, but removed it long enough to ask, "Am I bleeding?" I reassured him he was not bleeding, but there was a large round reddened area on his right temple. He noted that at the same moment he had been "hit," the sander had stopped operating and wondered if perhaps a short circuit in the machine had caused the blow. But this seemed unlikely because the short would have had to detour his arm and jump through the air to hit him in the temple only, and besides electrical shocks wouldn't be likely to make a localized bruise.

We quickly made our way downstairs to find our poor harassed electrician and asked him if such a thing were possible. He backed away warily and said "No." Then I asked him if he would please repair the sander. He took it apart, could find no problem, turned it on—it worked. He replaced the casing, turned it on—it didn't work! He took it off again, looked at it, turned it on—it worked. He replaced the casing, turned it on—it wouldn't work! This pattern continued for several more times. Later, I was delighted to see a professional union electrician sitting, spraddle-legged, beating the sander repeatedly against the floor. He was the picture of frustration, I chided him that I thought that was the way only we amateurs fixed things.

The rental sander was returned still unoperable for no apparent reason. Tom completed his work and has been gone for years, but we have heard stories that our bewildered electrician still enlivens his conversation among co-workers with stories of his days at Bradmar.

By this time word of the strange doings at Bradmar had reached the ears of a newspaper feature-writer, Mr. Bernard Kelley of *The Denver Post.* He included this material in an article "So You Don't Believe in Ghosts," appearing in a Sunday supplement, *Contemporary Magazine,* dated October 28, 1962.

Chapter 4

Do All Humans
Have E.S.P.?

Before launching into our theoretical ex-
planations for the various physical phenomena described thus far,
we should review Dr. Bradley's background since it has much to
do with the development of these theories.

As a Doctor in post-graduate specialty training at the University of Minnesota in 1947, I became very intellectually curious
about the function of the human brain compared with the brains of
other animals. This curiosity was first aroused by the work of the
late Dr. Grantly Dick-Read of England, suggesting that human
animals are non-instinctual but could function on an instinctive
level if properly trained. Every adult animal on earth falls into
deep water and instinctively swims—except the human animal (he
has to be taught what to do in water). The pregnant wild animals
go peacefully about the business of giving birth to their young
when they enter labor. Apparently only the human does not know
what to do in labor and must be "delivered" of his young under
anesthetics.

Assuming that the poor ignorant human was non-instinctual,
I have as an obstetrician, had the privilege since then of training
over 7,000 husbands, enabling them to coach their wives to
carefully imitate other animals in their conduct during labor,
resulting in human mothers joyfully giving birth to their young
without risks of depressions due to anesthetics. This method is

called "Natural Childbirth" and is another story in its own right described in detail in another book, *Husband-Coached Childbirth*.[1]

Dr. Dick-Read's theories were sound, and put into practice and enlarged a bit, formed the basis for an entirely new concept of psychosomatic obstetrics.

Some puzzlers in human instinct

But there were puzzling questions that kept cropping up in my work. An occasional human mother seemed to know how to act in labor without being taught! An occasional adult human fell into deep water and swam without previous training! Apparently an occasional human "animal" *did* have instinct. Why don't they all? What is instinct? How is it manifested in animals? in humans? Why does it show up only sporadically in humans? Could it be that all humans do have inherent instinct but that it becomes manifest only under certain circumstances? Why? Where in the brain is instinctual function located? Has the human—as a more highly evolved animal—somehow lost brain function that the lower animals still retain?

Human and animal brains

Let's brainstorm a bit about these questions. Let's take a long look at human brains, anatomically first, and compare what we find with the brains of so-called "lower" animals. The first thing that becomes obvious is that the inner portion of the human brain closely resembles that of the entire brain of animals. It's the outer shell, the bark or cortex that looks different, is thicker and more complex in humans. There is only one animal reported with a thicker cortex or outer layer than the human, the dolphin. Too, like the human, it has nearly fifty percent of its brain mass consisting of the cortex. Other "lower" animals' cortices are, proportionately, extremely thin.

This outer layer is considered to contain the functions of the conscious, logical, abstract reasoning mind, those functions which are so highly developed in the human that other animals occupy cages in zoos, while humans build huge cities, rockets to the moon, etc. After reading Dr. Lilly's book on the dolphins, I believe it to be entirely possible that the dolphins' highly developed complex

---

[1]Robert A. Bradley, *Husband-Coached Childbirth* (New York: Harper & Row Publishers, Inc., 1965).

cortices enable them to be similarly advanced in their environment, the sea. I personally think that dolphins are more highly evolved in water than we are on land—they never hurt each other (or humans), but are noted for coming to each other's aid (and to the aid of humans!). We humans have yet to achieve such a high plane!

Now let's drop the study of the outer part—the cortex—which looks different, and dwell on the inner part of the human brain in comparison with other animals. The first thing that strikes us is—it looks so similar. This area of the brain is sometimes referred to as the older brain or animal brain. If it looks similar, the next logical question is, could it be similar in function?

On the basis of the similarity of appearance between the *inner* portion of the human brain and the *entire* brain of lower animals and for convenience of study, I wish to propose a theory. The theory is admittedly greatly over-simplified, but I hope it will serve to provoke further investigation into a more academic study of the comparison between animal-human brain functions.

This theory is that the animal brain has very little, if any, conscious brain function that compares with the human. Other animals are said not to be self-conscious. They apparently cannot abstractly think, reason, utilize symbols for ideas, etc. Their behavior is "animal" in nature unless trained otherwise, and this training—superimposed by humans—is effective on a conditioned reflex basis rather than on a reasoning, thinking, logical basis. Their conscious brain function, if any, produces little, if any, restriction upon their animal behavior. They act instantly and instinctively in response to fear, anger, sex, hunger, etc., without apparent conscious brain activity to limit, restrict, or inhibit in any way these basic animal drives.

Humans, on the other hand, have conscious reasoning brain function which over-lays, restricts, and inhibits these basic instinctual drives. We don't gobble our food "like an animal"; we don't act uninhibited sexually; we learn to suppress our tempers; we cover up our fear, etc. Could this complex conscious portion of human brains be "covering-up," smothering, interfering with and partially blocking other instinctual functions of the animal portions of our human brain, functions other than the obvious ones listed?

The theory, then, is this—that human brains have retained in their evolutionary development an animal portion which fully functions comparably to the brains of lower animals. However, because of the dominance of the complex superimposed conscious portion of human brains, these animal instinctual functions are, for the most part, smothered or covered-up and become manifest on a "sub-conscious" level in humans.

Animals, on the other hand, neither have nor need this two-leveled type of awareness. They function entirely on the same level that in humans is restricted to the sub-conscious. This is probably purposeful in animals and, in their predatory existence, is life saving, for it enables them to be more acutely perceptive of danger and to act immediately and instinctually without the handicap of delaying action due to conscious processing.

This sub-conscious or animal brain in humans is made manifest by "breaking through" to a conscious level spontaneously, occasionally. It can also break through due to extreme stress, emotions, dire necessity, prolonged fasting, prolonged silence (used by the Russians in brain washing at subconscious levels), and prolonged restriction to cramped quarters (Charles Lindbergh during his famous flight). It can be evoked in religious meditation, traumatic shock, and, more recently, demonstrated by the chemical action of drugs known as psychedelic or consciousness-expanding drugs.

Could increased awareness of our animal brain functions be put to practical use, enabling us to better understand ourselves and others? Would such awareness enable us to better meet the stresses of this life without emotional crippling from unrecognized subconscious-conscious conflicts? Such conflicts represent the basis of most personality disorders in humans. Could more knowledge of our sub-conscious animal brain result in practical utilization of these too long-ignored functions to make our lives more meaningful?

Let's consider some functions of the animal brain other than the emotions mentioned previously and compare them with our own. For convenience and simplicity let's divide these other functions into categories or pigeonholes to discuss and compare them more easily.

Instinctual function No. 1—How to act in water

Animals—Animals in nearly all species know well how to act in water. There are perhaps a few exceptions (e.g., polar bear) in which the mother animal seemingly needs to teach the young. But who taught the *first* polar bear mother?

Humans—If you drop a hundred adult humans in deep water for the first time, probably over 90% would drown. Now we find a thought-provoking fact: if you drop a hundred human babies *prior to the age of six months* in deep water for the first time, over 90% would swim! Why do more human *babies* manifest instinct than human *adults*? Could learning, acquiring knowledge, and adjusting to the stresses of life possibly serve to cover-up or interfere with subconscious human instinct?

Instinctual Function No. 2—How to act in labor

Animals—Again, all animals know how to act in labor. No doctor has to drag anesthetic machines into the woods to put mother foxes, wolves, coyotes, sheep, etc., to sleep, take steel pliers and pull their young from them—they peacefully give birth. A young farm mother came to our office with her first pregnancy to be taught natural childbirth because she watched a cow have a calf and she swore the cow smiled as it gave birth! The lady was half joking but I understood, because I too had seen the shiny radiant look in an animal mother's eyes at the birth of its young.

Humans—If left alone, unenlightened, untrained as to the proper procedure, 90% of women in labor cry out in pain from tensing and holding back and eventually have to be *delivered*. Why do they have to be taught how to act so that their baby can be *born*?

When they are carefully taught and lovingly coached by trained husbands (see book), 94% give birth joyfully, as do animals, without medication or forceps. Moreover, like the other animals, they do not "get sick" and they walk about, immediately after giving birth.

But what about the 10% or so that peacefully work with the forces of labor without prior indoctrination and give birth as animals do? My mother gave birth to eleven pounds of me, at home without drugs, and kidded the doctor because *he* perspired and she didn't and he didn't do anything—*she* did all the work! She felt sorry for the poor perspiring doctor, got up and made him a cup of coffee!

Could serenity from deep religious faith thin, or part, the clouds of conscious fears and anxieties allowing in these occasional mothers true, deep instinctual drives to properly function? Indeed, indeed it can, and often does—others need to be trained and coached.

Instinctual Function No. 3—Hibernation

Animals—Certain lower animals demonstrate the instinctive ability to adapt their bodies and minds to the cycle of available-unavailable food and to the cycle of tolerable-intolerable weather conditions. This special winter-sleep state of hibernation includes insects, reptiles, certain fishes, frogs, toads, snails, the horseshoe crab; and as we come up the scale of animals, partial hibernation is performed by the prairie dog and squirrel, and typical total hibernation by the marmot and bear.

The aquatic forms bury themselves in the mud on the beds of streams during the winter months; the terrestial ones burrow into the ground below the level of frost and await the return of spring. Caterpillars remain hidden under the bark of trees or under moss and become solidly frozen and brittle. They gradually thaw out in the spring and return to "life." If the warmth returns too rapidly, many of them die.

The state of suspended animation of bodily processes in, for example, the bear, is brought about by deliberate if not conscious mind-body control. This long, long period of apparent "sleep" does not actually resemble the usual state the body assumes during nocturnal rest periods; hibernation is different. In order to survive over such a long period of time on a limited food supply the hibernating animal must alter bodily metabolic functions. The heart is made to beat more slowly, the circulation is slowed, the respiration is reduced so that oxygen requirements are minimal. Body temperature gradually reduces to nearly that of the environment.

In addition to the deliberate setting-back of the *body* regulator to such a slow, idling speed, there must be a similar and simultaneous slowing down of the processes of the *mind* or the animal would become restless and "stir crazy" from such long confinement and immobility. This alteration of *mental* function is also efficiently accomplished and the animal is said to be in a trance-like state, as required by the circumstances.

Humans—What does hibernation ability have to do with human "animals?" Can humans hibernate? Do they need to or want to? The answer to these two questions may surprise you: it is "yes" to each. Humans *can* alter their body functions similarly. This has been demonstrated ably by certain yogis who by self-hypnosis and deep meditation deliberately alter their metabolism, slow down all their bodily processes for a set period of time allowing themselves to be literally buried alive in a box in the ground and dug up days or even weeks later. Their bodies function on less food and less oxygen during this time, and their minds are "turned down" to a state of repose that is described as refreshing, restful, and beneficial. We are humans but we are also basically animals.

Some years ago a yogi demonstrated on a television program how he could actually stop his heart from beating for a few minutes as well as deliberately slow down its rate of beating. This was made visible to the audience by an electrocardiographic set-up in which the beat of the heart was visibly registered by the movements of the instrument's needle on a graph.

Do humans need to hibernate?

Now, the second question, "Do humans need to or want to hibernate?" is illustrated by an advertisement in our local newspaper recently stating that a fee would be paid by the University of Colorado to anyone bringing in live marmots. The hibernation ability of these animals is being studied with reference to possible human hibernation as a part of travel in space by future human astronauts. The learning of instinctual performances by humans is not limited to swimming and giving birth!

Interplanetary space travel involves human beings "holed-up" in confined areas (space ships) for long periods of time (probably years) and requires that they subsist on greatly diminished supplies of oxygen and food. If these astronauts can be trained like the yogis by self-hypnosis enabling them to alter their bodies and minds to adapt to these conditions of confinement, to adapt to this environment, then human space travel will be possible. One white crow means that all crows aren't black. One yogi demonstrating human hibernation means that humans are basically animals. If one can do it, why can't others? They can and the future will show that they will.

Let's brainstorm into the future a little more here. If caterpillar flesh can be solidly frozen during the winter and come back to full activity when slowly thawed, is it possible that human flesh can be preserved? We have already developed human bone banks, eye banks, and an enterprising and very serious group now offer cryogenic crypts wherein, for a tidy sum of money, you can have your body remain in a frozen state until organ transplant techniques become further developed so that the part that wore out in your body (heart, lung, kidney, liver, etc.) can be replaced by a good "spare." Your body can be thawed out (slowly!) like the caterpillars to function again, later on. Incredible? Yes. Impossible? Well, who knows?

Instinctual Function No. 4—Memory

Animals—The elephant's prodigious memory is traditional, but other species also have remarkable memories. Hates, loves, behavior patterns, etc., learned in early life become manifest many years later.

Humans—How about the animal portion of the human brain? Does it too have a remarkable memory? Yes it does. Carefully recorded in the subconscious, as if by a tape recorder, is every previous human experience. This recording is replayed under various circumstances:

1. In normal sleep and dreams.

Here is vivid reliving of past events, detailed and utilizing all the familiar senses—sight, sound, touch, taste, and smell. So convincingly real are these dreams that it is sometimes hard to "get back" to conscious reality upon awakening.

2. Electrical stimulation of the brain.

As a young medical student years ago, I was supposed to be learning about neurosurgical treatment of epilepsy. I was helping to hold steady the head of an unanesthetized (except for novacaine on the scalp) patient while the neurosurgeon explored his exposed brain with an electrical stimulating needle seeking the damaged area. Instead of observing the surgeon's technique in attempting to reproduce the epileptic seizure, my attention was drawn to the behavior of this adult as the electrical needle wandered about his brain. He would talk and act like a young child, then—as the current was stopped—come bewilderedly back to the present and tell us how he had been living past events.

The fact that electro-magnetism is involved in the mechanics of the reliving function of the brain was mentioned, seriously, on a television program recently by researchers looking into the future.

They suggested that electromagnetic recording of these neurological memory impulses could be picked up and preserved on magnetic tapes and we could "replay" from our library any recorded past experiences at will. What a way to spend a future rainy evening!
3. By suggestion under hypnosis.

Hypnosis will be dealt with in detail in a later chapter but mention must be made here of the technique of revivification or age regression. This consists of a replaying via suggestions of the brain's "tape recording" of previous experiences in the altered state of awareness called hypnosis. Superficially, the inexperienced may scoff that this is only acting out a role on the part of an ingratiating cooperative subject. Let me assure you that although a good actor may try, it is obvious when being acted and obvious when real, to experienced medical hypnotists.

As an illustration—a fellow doctor was age-regressed to test out the startle reflex. This is another manifestation of the change in human brain function that occurs at about age six months. *After* six months of age—if suddenly given the startling feeling of falling—humans will simply and reflexly reach out to grasp something for support to prevent the fall. They have learned by conditioned reflex what comes next. *Prior* to age six months infants do not make any attempt to grasp for support but will merely bawl and wet their diapers when startled.

Our doctor friend was placed in a reflex chair that could be suddenly released to drop backward for a short distance, giving the sudden feeling of falling. In the age-regression experiment, until he was back to six months of age, he would simply try to grasp something for support. When regressed younger than six months of age and the button was pushed tipping the chair, he made no effort to catch himself but reacted true to expectations! What an actor!

In the practical application of medical hypnosis to correct human behavior problems, age regression is of primary importance as will be shown later. The past affects the present and the future in many ways.
4. By drugs and medication.

The brain's tape recording of previous events can also be replayed by the chemical effect of drugs on the brain.

These drugs are known as psychedelic or hallucinogenic drugs and knowledge of their function and use is in its infancy. One of the many effects is vivid recall and reliving of past events. Keep your eye on them. These drugs are destined to play an important role in human behavioral science for they "expand" the conscious brain to become aware of the subconscious.

Instincutal Function No. 5—Telepathy or mind reading

We are now considering mind function categorized as E.S.P. (extra sensory perception) and known for centuries to be operating in lower animals and accepted blindly by the public as just one of those things peculiar to animals. The possibility that these functions may also operate in human animals has been mostly ignored, shunned, or left to a group I prefer to call "psychoceramics" or crack-pots. This is a pity, for in the haystacks of fraud, "magic," and trickery are to be found needles of reality for those who would seek them out. The bright light of academic research has yet to be turned fully upon this field, but it will, it will, probably as a result of jealousy over the interest and work of Russian scientists in this field as a possible aid to communication between astronauts. Let's consider this instinctual function—the ability to perceive thoughts by other than usual communicative channels—telepathy.

Animals—Intraspecies (between same species) communication between animals of the same or similar type is illustrated by a pack of wolves planning and executing a complicated relay method of tiring a pursued elk. One wolf seems to know instantly what the other plans on doing and acts accordingly. This is also illustrated quite simply in watching a school of fish swimming along. They will all make identical sudden turns simultaneously. How do they know instantaneously what the others plan on doing? Pertinent again is Dr. Lilly's fascinating story of the dolphins, the story of how whales communicated immediately to other whales over a huge area of the sea the knowledge to avoid ships with mounted harpoon guns. After one whale had been injured the whales for a radius of hundreds of miles instantly avoided ships with harpoon guns but freely swam near ships of similar appearance without guns. How do they let each other know such detailed information? Inter-species (between different species) telepathic communication can also be illustrated with many examples. Dr. Lilly needed only to think the usually spoken command to achieve the dolphin response. There are innumerable records of animals howling, refusing to eat, etc., coincident with the death of their beloved masters, even though separated by great distances. As any mailman can verify, there is a telepathic reception between human and dog. Dogs seem to know whether you are afraid of them or not, and act accordingly.

One lady in our study group told of her grandfather trying to shoot a crow that roosted in a tree near his cornpatch. When he had a loaded shotgun the crow would exasperatingly fly away just before he intended to shoot. One day he had no shells but took the gun along to frighten the crow. The insolent crow merely sat, looked at him, and "crowed." This was repeated many times and the crow always flew away if the gun was loaded, and stayed if it wasn't. How did the crow know what he knew? We don't know *how* but we certainly know *that* it knew.

Humans—There is not a thinking open-minded human on earth who has not had some personal experience illustrating that he could perceive the thoughts of others. This is usually manifested more often between people who are emotionally attached (mother-child, husband-wife, close friends, etc.) but one Mr. Dunninger would chuckle heartily if I should imply that it can't be done between strangers—he's been doing it in public demonstrations for years.

My wife and I receive thought impressions regularly between us. We were reading silently in the library the other night when each of us began humming the identical old tune at the identical place. How often have you had the impression that someone would call—to have the phone ring and there they are. Mere coincidence? Hardly. There are too many of these cases.

Shortly after our young nephew's experience of knowing the contents of Christmas packages, I came home late for dinner, as happens often to practicing obstetricians. The family members were all dining, and normally I would have joined them. On this evening, however, I was tired after a long day and was thinking to myself as I entered the door, no, I'll go turn on the fountain on the terrace and rest awhile before I eat. Mark jumped up and said, "No, let me do it, I want to do it!" He said, "I want to turn on the fountain. Let me do it!"

When queried how he knew I was going to turn on the fountain, he looked confused, "But you said you were." The others chimed in, "He didn't say anything!" To Mark, at that tender open age, a thought was as perceptible as a word—he couldn't tell the difference.

I have had the privilege of giving talks on the subject to many groups many times. The group I find most responsive and most rewarding when I ask for personal examples is the junior-senior group, from eight to sixteen years of age. I get flooded with examples. The uncluttered conscious minds of these young people do not block or interfere with the underlying subconscious functions.

One little girl, nine years of age, explained that she had a girl friend her age who lived next door. They were constant companions (it helps) and people mistook them for sisters. The preceding summer her friend had gone away to a ranch in Wyoming during the three-month school vacation. In early August of that summer the first young lady described how she was walking through the living room when she fell to the floor crying and sobbing because of a sudden pain in her right leg. She stated that her frightened mother called the doctor but (giggle) when he arrived the pain was all gone and she was fine. Later she discovered that her girl friend in Wyoming had fallen from a horse and broken her right leg in that identical spot, on that identical day, at that identical time!

A young boy in the group described how he had been riding to school with his father one morning when his father suddenly slumped over the wheel, acted as if he had suddenly gone to sleep, and allowed the car to run off the road. His father "came to" shortly and bewildered, got the car back on the road, wondering how on earth he could have done such a thing. They found out later that his brother had died of a heart attack at the wheel of his car in a distant city on the very same day at the very same time.

Hardly a talk goes by without interruption by squeals of recognition coming from the eager youngsters. This is especially true when I illustrate the ability of identical twins to perceive each others thoughts, aided perhaps not only by social and personal ties but also by genetic bonds. An aware, thinking, alert grade school teacher noticed that her young identical twin pupils took turns taking home books. On questioning them, she found her suspicions confirmed—they were taking turns studying, yet each passed the tests!

Two handsome, sixteen-year-old twin boys in one group described how they did the same and bragged that the twin who didn't study got the best grade on exams!

A football coach in a local high school described how he could never scrimmage twin boys on opposite teams. No matter what play was called the twin brother would know exactly where the ball player was going and tackle him immediately.

And so it goes, fact after fact, showing that the human animal does still retain instinctual function. Yet even as the stack of evidence grows higher and higher, even in this so-called advanced society, we still have scientific ostriches who bury their heads in the familiar sands of conformity, refusing to accept facts which do not comfortably fit into their preconceived pigeonholes of what they think ought to be, blindly rejecting what is. Let's adjust the pigeonholes to fit the facts, not vice versa!

Instinctual Function No. 6—Clairvoyance: seeing with the mind's eye

This function involves the brain's ability to visualize accurately actual physical objects by other means than the usual use of eyesight and direct vision.

Animals—The animal brain can visually perceive objects even at great distances and through great obstacles. This is probably the mechanism involved when animals return to an empty house that is home to them, a phemonenon well dramatized by Walt Disney in his movie *The Incredible Journey.* Two dogs and a cat return home over the Canadian wilderness in winter, even though the family members were all absent.

How do the animals know which turn in the road to take? The investigated evidential cases involving animals performing feats of this nature are so voluminous that they would fill several volumes.

Humans—Is the animal brain of human beings capable of seeing things at great distances, through any obstacle? By all means!

Here again the stack of verified evidential cases of human clairvoyance grows higher and higher. Here again the stimulus producing this ability is usually fraught with high emotional content. It isn't necessary, but it surely helps! Mothers "see" the actual wreck scenes involving injury or death to their children. During the inhumanity of wars, many mothers have described the actual scenes at the battlefield where theirs sons fell, much to the amazement of fellow soldiers. These sightings often occurred to the mother in dreams but some also occur in waking states. They all have one great factor in common, vividness and uncompromising reality. There is never any doubt in the mind of the perceiver that this event was actual.

Instinctual Function No. 7—Precognition, Prophecy, or Fore-knowledge

This function probably is only a further manifestation of those of telepathy and clairvoyance with variation in the element of *time*. Prophecy, however, has played such an important role in history that I feel it warrants a separate category.

What is time? No one knows for sure. One thing is obvious in our study—the subconscious mind is no respecter of *time*. Subconscious awareness can be of the present, the past, or the future, or all three scrambled together. This is illustrated by the activity of the subconscious in dreaming. Long past events are relived, but there may be persons or happenings of recent origin mixed into the activity.

Animals—Can animals predict an event before it occurs? In our study of instinct do we have examples of prophecy in the lower animals? Indeed, we have many.

For example: The tradition of the rats deserting a ship at the docking that preceded its sinking at sea. On an island, days prior to an earthquake, the eerie silence due to the birds flying away and deserting the area before disaster occurs.

The recent Alaskan earthquake and tidal wave provides another example of animal precognition, as described in the newspapers. A herd of cattle follow a set grazing pattern, as fellow country dwellers well know. A particular herd in Alaska were noted to change their pattern the morning that preceded the earthquake and tidal wave. Had the herd maintained its usual pattern the cows would have been caught in the low-lands at the time the tidal wave occurred and would have perished. They had knowingly reversed their pattern so they were safe on the higher ground at the time of the disaster.

I was being interviewed on a local television program (Bill Barker's, *Hot Topic,* Channel 4) and we were discussing evidence of animal precognition. At the end of the program the cameraman took me aside and added another example to the list. He described how his presence, his very life, was due to such instinctual awareness manifested by a herd of cattle. During the war he and a comrade were trapped on an island that was being bombarded by the enemy. Not knowing where the shells would land they were at a loss as to how to protect themselves until they inadvertently observed the activities of a herd of cattle. They noticed that the cattle would be grazing peacefully, then, suddenly, they would all hurriedly change to another area. Shortly after the move an artillery shell would land where they had just been. He attributed his survival to this observation. He and his comrades utilized this knowledge and joined the herd.

At a talk I was giving to a service club, a native of Costa Rica was present as a guest. He volunteered the information that natives who lived near an active volcano in Costa Rica had time to get to higher ground and safety because their domesticated animals characteristically knelt down with their heads between their forelegs awaiting the ground-shaking eruption of the volcano. They seemed to precognitively know approximately fifteen minutes in advance that the eruption would occur.

Again, we do not know *how* animals can do this, but let's quit ignoring the fact *that* they can.

Humans—Is there evidence of human animal brains functioning precognitively? History is loaded with such evidence. The oracles of Biblical days were not only highly esteemed but utilized regularly for their abilities. Hardly any ruler was so rash in his decisions as not to consult first the oracles and prophets for guidance on future policies.

Are such talented people limited to Biblical days? Not at all. Jeanne Dixon is one well-known current prophetess who has played an important role on the political scene, accurately predicting many things, including President Kennedy's assassination, Dag Hammarskjöld's death, etc. For an excellent review of present day oracles see the book by Jess Stearns, *The Door to the Future*.[2] Mr. Stearns, a professional writer, set out to "expose" this type of fraud, and as has happened so many times, his honest investigation resulted in an alteration of not only his thinking but his writing and his living as well.

Do we have to pick isolated examples to illustrate human precognition? Again, there is not an open-minded human on earth who has not occasionally had glimpses of this function. It may be manifest as merely a vague feeling of uneasiness or dread that preceded bad news. At a talk I gave to a businessmen's club a member of the club described how one afternoon he'd left the office in mid-afternoon and gone hurriedly home. He didn't know the reason for his action but had the non-ignorable urge to go

---

[2]Jess Sterns, *The Door to the Future* (Garden City, N.Y.: Doubleday & Co., Inc., 1963).

home. He had a dread that something was wrong with one of his two children.

When he arrived home he asked where the children were. His wife said that one was playing in the back yard and the other at the neighbor's. A few minutes later the neighbor's child came running with the awful news that their child had accidentially strangled himself with a rope during play.

His wife kept repeating "I knew it, I knew it" while they ran to the scene. He later asked her to explain this statement. She told him that she had been dreaming a recurrent dream for a year that this child would be killed!

A practicing physician related a very vivid dream he'd had that a certain pregnant patient had given birth to her baby. At the time of his dream the patient was not actually due to have her baby for several months, but the dream was so shocking and disturbing in its reality that the next morning he had described it in detail to his office nurse. In the dream the baby had congenital absence of its eyeballs as well as bilateral hare-lip and was quite disturbing in appearance. At the actual birth a few months later the doctor was shocked to see the exact scene he had visualized in his dream. This extremely rare abnormality had been clearly foretold by precognitive clairvoyance of the doctor's subconscious mind.

In a newspaper there appeared a reproduction of a bank check made out by a well-known rodeo performer. He had cashed the check at a restaurant just before boarding a plane and under his signature had written the word "heaven" on the line calling for his address. A short time later he died in the crash of the plane at Salt Lake City, Utah. He had consciously joked about what he had written, but his subconscious was not joking!

Not all precognitive dreams involve dreadful or abnormal happenings. Some can be rather amusing. For instance, a physician's wife laughingly told us at a dinner party of a vivid dream she had had. She dreamed of herself accompanied by her young son standing in line at a cashier's window in her local bank. She saw her young son come up to her in the line munching on something and in the dream she remonstrated with him, not knowing what it was or where he got it, and she told him to "Spit it out, immediately!" Then, as her turn came at the cashier's window, she heard a man's voice just next to her say "Stick 'em up!" She awakened in fright at being involved in a bank robbery.

A few days later she did go to the bank to make a deposit. Her young son was with her. As she was standing in line she looked up to see him munching on an apple he had apparently picked up somewhere and she indignantly told him to spit it out. As she said this she recalled her dream of a few nights before. At the same moment she heard a man's voice say "Stick 'em up!" and she let out a blood-curdling scream, threw her hands up, money and checks flying everywhere. The pretty girl teller calmly told the man, "O.K., I'll be ready for lunch in a minute." She shame-facedly retrieved her money and checks off the floor as everyone glared at her as if she were a silly, hysterical woman. The man, it seemed, was merely giving his girl friend, the teller, what he thought was his clever daily greeting as he stopped to accompany her to lunch.

Precognition becomes evident not only at the time of disaster. It may be a feeling that "I just knew" some particular person was going to call, or visit, etc., and, lo and behold, they do! Some people, blessed with extra sensitivity can learn to depend on these feelings.

The unclouded open minds of children do not process these feelings consciously or attempt to analyze them, they simply accept them and act upon them.

"Psi" experiences, or evidences of human instinct, seldom occur in just one category. As we stated at the opening of this chapter, precognition is not an entity unto itself, but more likely the element time acting in relationship to telepathy and clairvoyance.

Our nephew, Mark, also occasionally acts upon precognitive influences. When he was in first grade and had yet to acquire the ability to add beyond 2 + 2 = 4, he and the children were playing a complicated game called "cargo" involving the necessity of adding up long columns of figures to see who had won. He gave his aunt the figures to add and was impatiently awaiting the total figure. His impatience grew as the list was silently and laboriously added. Finally, he burst out, "Oh, it's $465,764.29." In a moment she completed the addition and was startled to find the total sum sounded familiar. She asked, "What did you say?" He repeated the number, and it was identical!

Once, when he was in the sixth grade, he came home from school fussing and indignant because some people never believe him. His school has occasional unexpected fire drills and he had been taught that his duty was to close the windows when the alarm sounded. He "knew" a drill was coming, had left his seat and began to close the windows. Since no alarm had sounded the teacher indignantly insisted he open them again. He had barely finished when the alarm did sound, just as he somehow knew it would.

The mother of another lad with similar instinctual abilities has described her child's irritation because adults don't believe him when he knows something is going to happen. This boy at age eight awakened early and disturbed his parents' sleep one morning a week *before* President Kennedy's death. The boy came crying and sobbing into their bedroom upset because President Kennedy had been killed. He excitedly told them to turn on the television, that everybody was talking about it. The parents were rather irritated and brusquely ordered him not to make up such horrible stories. A week later when it happend he wasn't interested in the news; he didn't even interrupt his play to grieve—he'd already been through all that!

Later on, his mother was cross with him when he asked her not to let his brother play with a certain neighborhood child. He said that the child was a bad boy and would get his brother in trouble. His mother criticized him sharply for saying such things about the young innocent-looking neighbor lad. However, a few days later, a policeman appeared at the door with his brother in tow; the "innocent" neighbor lad had taken a hammer and broken out headlights on a row of parked cars, and the brother got the blame. "When will you learn to listen to me!" His bewildered mother consulted me as a doctor thinking there was something "wrong" with her son. She left thinking there was something blessed and "right" with him. Perhaps the "wrong" element lies in the unaware adults, who unlike children do not immediately accept and act upon instinctual "feelings" and are forever doubting those who do. There are many more examples, but let's get on: we have so much to cover.

Instinctual Function No. 8—Visual Acuity or Subliminal Visual Perception

Animals—Can lower animals see more acutely than humans? Is the animal brain more sensitive to vision? Of course, it is even said that animals can see in the dark. Actually, not in total darkness. They can see more, and in dimmer light, than humans. This is too well known to dwell on.

Humans—If the animal brain is more perceptive to light, can that portion of the human brain, which looks like that of the animals (the subconscious) also visually "see" more than the conscious brain? As a matter of fact, it can and we even have a special label for this instinctual ability when applied to humans—subliminal visual perception.

Most of the material we are discussing would fall in the category of the non-tangible and is hard to reproduce under laboratory conditions of tangible testing. Subliminal visual perception, however, can be adroitly demonstrated by experimentation.

For instance—moving pictures. In the first place "moving" pictures is a misnomer—they don't move! They are a series of rapidly placed intermittent *still* pictures. They only appear to move due to the slow and sluggish nature of the visual perception of the human *conscious* mind. The conscious mind is noted for its logical reasoning, for its ability to abstract, etc., but it is ponderously slow by comparison to the subconscious in the field of visual perception. Moving pictures only *appear* to move. This illusion is created by taking advantage of the slowness of conscious perception. Could the disinterest shown by dogs and cats for "moving" pictures be related to the fact that they see intermittent, jerky, still pictures instead of the illusion of movement?

We have become accustomed to refer to our human subconscious mind as "George"—it gets tiresome to repeat that cumbersome word. "Let George do it" is no longer a trite suggestion, as it will become evident later in our discussion of psychosomatic medicine.

When one watches a "movie" the human conscious mind perceives the illusion of movement, but our "George" sees intermittent still pictures. How do we know? Because under laboratory conditions of testing suggestive signs were spliced in the movie film and not seen by the conscious mind (they flicked by too rapidly) but were indeed seen and acted upon by "George." The traditional experiment was an "Eat More Popcorn!" sign spliced intermittently into the film at a movie house and shown on alternate nights as a study of subliminal visual suggestion. "George" is illogical and suggestible—as any hypnotist knows—and acts upon suggestion without conscious awareness. On the alternate nights that the subliminal suggestion was shown, the percentage of popcorn sacks sold in relation to the ticket admission was far higher. Patrons were eating far more popcorn without consciously knowing why. Think what advertisers could do if turned loose with this gimmick! Wisely, there are now laws against the use of subliminal visual advertising on movies and television.

It has been rumored that the Russians used such techniques in "brain washing" captive prisoners of war—taking advantage of the illogical suggestibility of the "Georges" of our men, and the average American citizen's abysmal ignorance of his own mind functions.

Instinctual Function No. 9—Auditory Acuity or Subliminal Auditory Perception

Animals—Animals can also hear more acutely than the human conscious brain is capable of hearing. This auditory sensitivity is essential to survival in the wild animal kingdom even today. Everyone is familiar with the fact that his pet dog or cat hears very faint sounds as well as sounds out of range for conscious human perception. It is well known that animal brains are auditorily sensitive to a wider span or spectrum of sound frequency. Here is an excellent potential experiment that, as far as I know, has never been performed. Do human Georges also perceive sounds over a wider frequency than human conscious minds? Is a human in a hypnotic trance more aware auditorily? Can age regression under hypnosis pick up subconscious awareness of previously heard sounds that were out of conscious range? Let's go on from ESP cards; there are great open unexplored territories staring us in the face!

Humans—The prehistoric human probably relied like other animals on his more acute *subconscious* hearing in order to survive among predators. In this modern age there is no particular motivation to be so acutely aware of faint sounds. However, if our life depended on this, we would probably still be as capable as other animals!

One of the most fascinating aspects of our George is that it is the only bodily function (subconscious awareness) that never needs to rest. The conscious mind, like muscle and nerve function, must have intermittent rest periods (sleep) in order to continue functioning. George never sleeps and apparently is not dependent upon chemical functions similar to the rest of the body. Could this be a facet of the soul, distinctly separate and not really dependent on the bodily functions? More on this hypothesis later.

Your George hears continuously, even while the conscious mind is sleeping. A moment's reflection would verify this.

George can be conditioned to responsibility. Being an obstetrician, I never allow my phone to ring twice at night. My George prods my conscious mind to wakefulness immediately—get to work!

Through the years my wife has slept peacefully through the phone's ringing. She doesn't consciously know it rings. But, as a mother, when the children fuss and cry out at night her George awakens her immediately. I've never heard them (consciously) myself!

Now this ability to hear subconsciously while consciously asleep was utilized during the War, when time was so precious, to aid in teaching oral-aural skills in foreign languages for training of spies. The method is referred to as "sleep teaching."

The men would not consciously recall the night's lesson but would learn it consciously far more rapidly and retain it better having previously been exposed to it subconsciously during sleep.

The subconscious human mind also hears and reacts even under the chemical effects of surgical anesthesia. The conscious mind is asleep but apparently George never sleeps. This has been ably reported in multiple articles in the medical pioneering work of David B. Cheek, M.D.[3] His studies pointed out that the subconscious mind remembers and recognizes statements that are made and ideas of deceit, anxiety, etc., but, significantly, never humor or joking. Humor is not truly an "animal" function but is peculiar to the human conscious brain. The human animal is the only one that laughs but not with its "animal" subconscious brain. Joking and humor is a product of human consciousness. I recall the jolt of awareness that struck my previously uncomprehending brain as I listened to this doctor's excellent presentation at a convention of medical hypnotists a few years ago.

I had just done a post-operative check on a very obese lady whose uterus I had removed six weeks previously. Prior to the operation she had always been very gushy and effusive in her outspoken admiration for her doctor—often to the point of embar-

---

[3]David Bradley Cheek, M.D., "Unconscious Perception of Meaningful Sounds During Surgical Anesthesia as Revealed Under Hypnosis," *The American Journal of Clinical Hypnosis* (Vol. 1, No. 3, 1959).

rassing me. At the post-op check she was completely the reverse in her attitude—surly, resentful, and withdrawn. At the convention I recalled with a shudder how I had pulled the "B.T.O." (big time operator) approach on a new intern who had assisted at this surgery. I had made flippant, sarcastic remarks about the thickness of the patient's abdominal fat and jokingly threatened to lower the intern down into the incision on a rope equipped with a walky-talky radio to keep me informed. After all, the patient was asleep from the anesthetic! She later felt uncomfortable and resentful in my presence. She didn't consciously know why, but if she were age-regressed under hypnosis, her George would tell you why, in a hurry!

Dr. Cheek reported on many cases of age regression under hypnosis reliving the experience of the surgery and revealing how the subconscious is continually aware of conversation and other sounds.

Believe me, I have spoken like a gentleman around anesthetized patients ever since. Their conscious minds may be asleep but their Georges are acutely aware and listening!

Instinctual Function No. 10—Touch—Subliminal Tactile Perception

Animals—This sense is more vague when applied to animals; we just have no real way of testing whether their sense of feel or touch is highly developed. One example may be the way salmon determine the minute changes in salinity of water at the mouth of rivers, enabling them to know when rain has fallen in the spawning grounds at the origin of the streams and signalling the beginning of their arduous trip.

Humans—There are multiple reports of humans being able to "see" via their skin or sense of touch—even determining colors and figures accurately. Is the skin a true sense organ which could be developed to function more astutely? Could there also be subliminal tactile perception? Here is another unexplored frontier.

Instinctual Function No. 11—Smell—Subliminal Olfactory Perception

Animals—The phenomenal ability of many animals to perceive faint scents undetectable to human noses is well known.

Humans—This is another unexplored frontier. I have not read or heard of subliminal olfactory studies in the human. I have been impressed by the vivid descriptions of fragrances and odors experienced by patients in hypnotic trances and quite frequently as a part of the experiences in spiritual seances.

Instinctual Function No. 12—Subliminal Gustatory Perception?

Here we draw a blank. I know of no experiments in the gustatory field, but who knows what the future may reveal?

Instinctual Function No. 13—Genetic Memory

Classification of instinctual functions as clear-cut divisions is really impossible. We are probably discussing overlapping functions of the same fundamental process anyway.

In this category, genetic memory, which is somewhat of a wastebasket, we will place many facets of instinct.

By genetic memory we refer to the carry-over from one generation to the next of knowledge or behavioral patterns. This is probably related to other inherited aspects, such as physical characteristics, and is probably carried from parent to progeny via similar genes and chromosomes.

Animals—The obvious examples of genetic memory in animals include:

1. The Monarch butterflies off the coast of California. The progeny are hatched out elsewhere but faithfully return to the same location, even the same tree, from which their parents originated. How do they know where it is?

2. The swallows that return to Capistrano are said to be progeny returning to the haunts of their parents.

3. The late Henry Ford was reputed to feel that chickens carry over memory to their young. He noticed shortly after inventing his flivver that the chickens on the farm when frightened by the approaching car would run *into* its path and be killed. The next generation, though, would run *away* from the car's path.

4. Nesting habits of birds—How do they know the complicated techniques of nest construction?

5. Preservation of species—the urge to reproduce. Hardly limited to lower animals—thank God!

6. Self preservation—flight or fight instinct.

Humans—Genetic memory in humans, of course, could be equally illustrated by (5) and (6) of animals.

A television show of a few years ago presented a program dramatically illustrating further evidence of genetic memory in humans. The incident involved a young couple who met at a summer resort which neither person had ever visited before. They became strangely attracted to each other, discovered that each realized what the other was going to say before he spoke. They both knew what was coming next around the turn of a path where neither had previously been. The puzzle was cleared up when it was found that each had a parent who had similarly met at this same location and had identical experiences here many years before these young people were born.

The possibility of other incidences of genetic memory is involved but clouded by the overlapping of explanations. For instance: a lady describes how as a nine-year-old girl she startled an attendant at a museum by insisting that live snakes should be in a particular display case because they "were before." This was true but it had been some twenty years before. They had not been using live animals since then, and this particular case had housed them. Her parents had visited the museum in those days and she cited this as an example of genetic memory. Of course, retro-cognitive clairvoyance, telepathic message from the parent's memory, etc., would also explain this case.

Deja vu phenomenona—a feeling of having experienced something before—are also examples with mixed explanations possible. The familiarity of a view, a stranger, an idea, a voice, etc., could conceivably be accounted for by genetic memory from a parent's experience. This well-known phenomenon will be dealt with more fully later.

Chapter 5

Psychokinesis—
Is a Thought a Thing?

If objects can affect a mind, as illustrated in evidence of clairvoyance, can this process be reversed? Can the mind affect objects? Is a thought a material thing that can act upon another material thing and cause a physical effect?

Evidently it can. Such action has been labeled psychokinesis or telekinesis. This concept is so important to us humans and is so necessary in considering possible explanations for the physical phenomena described at Bradmar that we have allotted it a separate chapter.

It could be another instinctual function but we have no way of knowing whether it occurs in lower animals. It may be peculiar to humans and represents in humans our 14th instinctual function.

The ability of thoughts to affect things is manifested in many ways. Let's consider a few:

1. ESP dice experiments

The ESP cards were replaced by automatically rolled dice by the academic parapsychologists at Duke Univeristy and elsewhere. Clairvoyant experiments were done wherein no human mind knew consciously the sequence of the way the dice fell. Students with higher than average "Psi" ability were assigned predetermined numbers of combinations to "think" or concentrate on, to see if the machine-rolled dice would fall in this combination higher than chance expectation. Positive results were obtained, varying with the student involved.

Could the fervent gambler by practice and mental concentration make dice "talk"? While I struggled tediously at menial extracurricular jobs to work my way through medical school, a classmate lived in luxury working his way as a professional gambler. Could the occasions when even amateurs are "red hot" and can seemingly make the dice do their bidding represent moments of increased psychokinetic ability?

Our nephew who manifested telepathy, clairvoyance, and precognition is a dangerous opponent with the dice in the game of parcheesi!

2. Mental force for physical action

At a Spiritual Frontiers Convention, Dr. Harmon Bro described how a well-known psychometrist Peter Hurkos had demonstrated his psychokinetic power by an experiment wherein by mental concentration he caused a water faucet to turn on until water dripped and then, again by mental assignment, caused it to shut off. This was done as a planned experiment in the presence of Dr. Bro. The experiment was not to be used as a regular means of turning on and off water faucets but rather to demonstrate Mr. Hurkos' power of concentration and to show that thoughts when controlled can affect things.

3. Thoughts affecting the growth of plants

Multiple experiments have been performed in the laboratory under controlled conditions demonstrating the increased or decreased rate of growth of various plants where the only variable was controlled thoughts directed towards the plants. One such experiment was performed in a Texas high school and a picture appeared in our local newspaper of the plant box, in this case young tomato plants growing from seeds in a hot box. The rows of plants given "positive" growth thoughts were higher and healthier than the rows given "negative" thoughts although the soil, water, and ultraviolet light, etc, were identical.

The little old widow who has outlived her loved ones and her human friends, in her loneliness makes friends out of her green growing plants. She talks to them, has endearing names for them, literally loves them. She is said to have a "green thumb." Could her thoughts affect the plants?

In a discussion of the effect of mental powers on plants, the matter of spiritual powers being involved cannot be ignored, although this subject has been saved for subsequent chapters. One cannot ignore the pioneering experiments of Reverend Lewis L. Dunnington, Minister of the First Methodist Church in Iowa City, who demonstrated for his congregation the power of prayer on plants by utilizing seeds planted in soil in pans placed on his pulpit. Also to be noted are the experiments and book[1] describing them by Rev. Franklin P. Loehr.

4. Thoughts affecting photographic film

Our first acquaintance with this possibility was the description in Anderija Puharich's *Beyond Telepathy*[2] of experiments with a Polaroid-Land Camera utilizing Peter Hurkos as the subject.

Quite recently in Bradmar's library and again, later, in the drawing room, Mr. Ted Serios of Chicago in a carefully controlled experiment quite clearly demonstrated his ability by mental concentration to project a thought image onto Polaroid film.

Ted was brought to our home by Dr. Jule Eisenbud, a medical colleague, eminent psychoanalyst, and pioneer investigator of psychic phenomena. Dr. Eisenbud was conducting a careful study[3] of pictures produced by Mr. Serios who simply stares into the camera and by strenuous concentration snaps the shutter open when he feels his mind is projecting the image. One can read about this type of thing (e.g., "Toronto Test of Ted Serios' Paranormal Photographs," by Alan Spraggett, *Fate,* July 1965) but to have it "brought home" to you before your eyes using your own camera and film, is most dramatic and effective.

Because of the haunted reputation of Bradmar, Ted was quite anxious to see whether he could get a "ghost picture." After several films showed just what one would logically expect

---

[1]Franklin Loehr, Rev., *The Power of Prayer on Plants* (Garden City, N.Y.: Doubleday & Co., Inc., 1959).

[2]Anderija Puharich, *Beyond Telepathy* (Garden City, N.Y.: Doubleday & Co., Inc., 1962).

[3]Jule Eisenbud, *The World of Ted Serios* (New York: Wm. Morrow and Co., Inc., 1967).

—blurred images of Ted's face close-up (he was using our Polaroid with a flash attachment) there then appeared an all black, then an all white print. Neither of these make sense as the camera was unchanged—set on infinity and held about a foot away from his face. Tension mounted in the observors. The next film showed a cloudy margin with a center picture of the front of a large building with Grecian columns and a small statue in a niche of the building. Dr. Eisenbud had just made a request to Ted before this shot was taken. He asked for a close-up of the statue seen the night before at a controlled session with some scientists. Lo and behold, this *was* a close-up of the previous view, or close enough to pass as such.

It is phenomenal enough to have *any* picture in focus on the film, but to have a target assigned and hit it seems truly super-human!

A few days later Ted performed again, this time in Bradmar's drawing room and got a clear view of what appeared to be the Washington monument but is still actually unidentified with leafy tree branches in the foreground. A second picture was obtained with a closer and sharper view of the same subject.

How is it possible to think images on a camera film? No one knows *how* but there was no doubt in the minds of the observers *that* it was accomplished by Mr. Serios, in our home, with our camera, in a well lighted room with us loading, unloading and developing our own film. These were only two occasions and four images. Ted has produced hundreds under the watchful eye of Dr. Eisenbud who is to analyze and report them as representative of the subconscious mind activity.

Isn't it a privilege to be living in an age where scientists are studying such fascinating aspects of human existence? Doesn't outer space exploration seem dim and dull when compared to the possibilities offered by exploring *inner* space?

Chapter 6

Independence of Soul

Can the human subconscious function independently of the body? Let us consider the following startling factors.

A. The lack of the need to rest

As mentioned under our discussion of subliminal auditory perception, *the subconscious hears not only more acutely than does the conscious mind but it does so continuously day and night, even during normal sleep.* It never seems to need rest. Why? Every other function of the human body is on a *rhythmical* basis. Work periods are followed by rest periods. This is true of muscle and nerve function in which fatigue inevitably takes its toll and a rest period must follow. Even the conscious mind must have its rhythmical periods of sleep and rest in order to continue functioning properly as disc jockeys in awake marathons find out.

The thought that perhaps the subconscious "sleeps" or is inactive while the conscious mind is awake, may occur to you. But this doesn't fit the facts. Telepathic messages, clairvoyant visions, etc., have occurred during wakeful periods as well as during sleep, probably in a higher incidence.

George (subconscious mind) seems to function continuously and has no spring that needs rewinding. From our present knowledge of bodily functions and metabolic processes this doesn't fit or seem possible. It can't be! But it is! Could it be that the human subconscious is not actually dependent upon the human body? That it functions along with, but actually can be totally independent of—the body?

The dependence of the conscious mind upon bodily function and the non-dependence of the sub-conscious is illustrated by the factor of body and brain impairment of function due to the degeneration of aging.

Not long ago, our little grandpapa passed away at close to the age of ninety years. He had resided in a home for the elderly and having had a heart attack, had been transferred to the hospital where he remained for a week before he died. Sieg and I were out to the home collecting his belongings from his room when a dear elderly lady there inquired as to his whereabouts. We gently explained that he had died and she exclaimed, "And I just saw him last night at the dinner table and we talked as we always do." We knew it was useless to try to correct her and straighten out in her mind that he had died over a week ago and had been away in the hospital for a week prior to that—she couldn't really remember *recent* events, just couldn't get them straight, but she could remember in accurate detail long ago, *past* events. These elderly people in hypnotic trances or merely from the altered awareness of their conscious minds caused by arteriosclerosis, will recount detailed events of the long past but can't tell you what happened yesterday. Recent memory is a conscious mind activity and is affected by bodily impairment. Memory of long past events is a subconscious mind activity not affected by bodily impairment, or even bodily death.

Bear this hypothesis in mind as we consider some other clinical observations of human mind-body relationships.

B. Spontaneous separation of mind from body in hypnotic trances

As a doctor I have for years used hypnotic trances in the office to utilize the subconscious minds of my patients for their own benefit in the treatment of frigidity, migraine headaches, functional infertility, marriage counseling, etc. A subsequent chapter will deal with this wonderful medical tool in detail. I bring it up here to drive an additional nail into the premise that the subconscious mind is not necessarily attached to the physical body.

Time and again I have treated women (who previously had never been consciously aware of this possibility) who have described to me in wonderment how during trances "they" were separate from their bodies and could see the consultation room scene, and their bodies, from a distant viewpoint.

I consistently give the suggestion early in trance that they will remember everything. I have never seen a medical advantage to amnesia, quite the contrary. I have been impressed through the years by the spontaneous descriptions of mind-body separation from patients who, as evidenced by their very bewilderment, were not previously cognizant of this possibility.

An indication of the increased awareness and public acceptance of the separability of the mind from the body was shown in an article that appeared in a recent edition of *The Wall Street Journal.* The article was titled "Beyond the Senses—Once Termed Fakery By Many, ESP Study Wins More Tolerance." It stated in part: "A 20-year-old girl believes she can leave her body as it sleeps and float to the ceiling. As an observer watches, she awakens after one such episode and accurately recites a five-digit number—written on a slip of paper by the observer and placed on a high shelf where she could not possibly have seen it."[1]

C. Evidences of unimpaired functions of the subconscious concomitant with practically non-function of the body (clinical body death)

We are aided here by the recent trend towards cardiac resuscitation and restoration of cardiac function after variable periods of the heart actually ceasing to beat. The latter comes from cardiac massage (external and/or internal) in heart attack victims and modern emergency rooms equipped with electrical cardiac stimulators and oxygenators, etc., to treat heart attacks more effectively and restore life after apparent physical death.

I recall an anesthesiologist at a convention describing how he was administering an anesthetic during a heart surgery operation. The patient was deeply asleep from his anesthesia. An intra-tracheal tube was in place in her windpipe, passing between her vocal cords, and a tight leak-proof fit had been obtained by inflation of a rubber cuff, to prevent drainage into the lungs of oral and nasal secretions.

The sutures in a large blood vessel unexpectedly gave way and before the surgeon could repair the "leak" the patient's blood

---

[1] "Beyond the Senses Once Termed Fakery By Many, ESP Study Wins More Tolerance," *The Wall Street Journal,* November 17, 1965.

pressure dropped to 0/0; she had no palpable pulse in her temples, her heart began vibrating (fibrillation) rather than pumping so that circulation of oxygen to her brain was cut off. She was in a state of deep shock just bordering on bodily death.

Her surgeon in a panicky voice asked whether anyone had seen her husband in the waiting room—"He should be warned we may lose her!"

The quiet of the operating room was broken by a deep muffled voice—"John's in the outer lobby!"—coming through the intra-tracheal tube from the patient herself! How could her George (her subconscious) be capable of this awareness and act upon it without oxygen and escape through the suppression of chemical anesthesia?

A cardiologist colleague of mine laughingly told me of a man he had done open-chest heart massage upon in the emergency room where he had been brought, from all appearances dead! After hours of work including all the tricks of his trade, they had re-established heart function. The laughter was occasioned the next morning on hospital rounds. As the doctor entered the room he overheard the patient's conversation. He had just been connected to his party on a phone call. His greeting to his friend on the phone: "Hey, Joe, guess what? I died last night! Yeah, really, no kidding, Joe!"

Apparently being restored from bodily death has in this age of cardiac treatment become such an accepted thing by the public that it is taken quite nonchalantly.

From cases of this nature careful inquiry done on the conscious level of what these people were thinking about, what they consciously remember during the time they were clinically dead, presents us with some additional data which illustrates again that impaired bodily function does not impair subconscious function.

The utilizable material from cases of this nature is skimpy because it represents only conscious remembering. This is like trying to recall what you were dreaming about—upon awakening from natural sleep. It's impossible for some, possible for others, and generally rather sketchy in detail. Let me express here a challenge to religious researchers; quit playing around with arm-chair philosophy and do a deliberate study via age regression under hypnosis of the *subconscious* awareness of those people brought back from clinical death! What a significant study this would be! With modern medicine the number is large enough now to be statistically valid!

The appearance of a consistent pattern

Even with access to only the conscious remembrance level we get a consistent pattern. These people describe their minds as being separate from their bodies. *They could see their bodies being worked on by the doctor and nurses.* They were aware of conversations going on about them and have startled the attendants by giving details of events and conversation that, being in a coma and *un*conscious, they logically could not have known, but actually did.

Moreover, these same "minds" would sometimes show a pattern of leaving the scene and traveling to distant points—going visiting—and could remember evidential details from distant scenes while their impaired bodies were being worked upon.

The one thing that they all stress is that their minds were not "in" their bodies during this crucial period. They speak *objectively* about their bodies until bodily function is re-established, then they describe, consistently, how they re-entered their bodies just before awakening, and again became "one" with their bodies and referred to themselves from a *subjective* aspect.

Another consistency that further suggests the separation of body and mind is their descriptions of the element of pain. They do not describe pain while separate, only upon re-entering the body. Pain is peculiar to bodily attachment.

After bodily death—what?

We are endowed with a human body at birth. This piece of mechanism consists of living flesh and like all living things runs the gamut, gradually wears out, and inevitably goes "the way of all flesh" ultimately back to a handful of inert chemicals. That which lives, forever dies, including thee and me!

The contemplation of this inevitable trip which we all must take plays a primary role in our behavior. No other trip we take will be as important or, from the evidence available, as adventurous as this one. Yet this is the one that most of us, like stupid ostriches, try to ignore, make no real preparation for, do not carefully plan in advance to meet our needs.

Why?

Philosophers and psychiatrists maintain that *the main cause of many personality disorders is the fear of death,* the fear of loss of personal identity, the fear that "I" will cease to be "me."

True relationship of mind to body

Let's take our ostrich heads out of the sands of escapism, ignore the taboo imposed by society and openly consider the available evidence of the true relationship of that all important "I" or "me" to this piece of modified clay we call a body.

We have established that the human subconscious mind shows evidence that although it is associated with the human body, it is not dependent upon it; that under stress of physical impairment, it can function separately; and that under altered states of awareness (hypnosis), the subconscious mind spontaneously may leave the body. There is, at least, an implication here which should prompt a question in any open, honest, logical, conscious mind. Does this awareness which manifests so vividly as "me" under these circumstances possibly continue unchanged as that same personal identity after the body has ceased to be? If it can function *temporarily* separated from the body, can it function *permanently* without the body?

Assuming it can, (and why not?) let's look around for some further evidence that it does. Do we have any available?

Evidence our mind continues after death

The evidence we have can only be circumstantial in nature since we cannot completely eliminate and isolate the activity of our subconscious mind from that of the persons who have survived bodily death. Such isolation has never been possible because of the wide sphere of action of the subconscious mind itself. There cannot be an isolated "only" label placed upon any effect even though it's considered to be due to one mind's action, since it is always *possible,* no matter how improbable, that another mind's action could have been involved.

Skeptics will laboriously follow complicated detours to reach the goal of a plausible explanation when a short, obvious, uncomplicated path lies directly before them.

This short path is represented by an hypothesis: *Subconscious minds do survive bodily death and maintain full activity.*

To illustrate this hypothesis, we itemized and discussed earlier a list of "instinctual functions" representing various abilities of the subconscious mind. Then we were describing and discussing subconscious minds in living animals, including the human, which are associated with conscious minds during bodily life.

Now, if we accept this hypothesis that the human subconscious mind can exist without the enveloping body and without the conscious portion of the now defunct brain, can we assume that the subconscious still retains all of these various functions we have listed? Without the attached body, the first three—how to act in water and in labor, and hibernation—become unnecessary since bodies are rather required for these functions. The other functions of the subconscious could conceivably still function without bodily attachment.

Here we come to an obstacle. Without a body these minds are in the realm of the intangible. They are referred to by the academic parapsychologists as "non-corporeal personal agencies."

Because of the intangible nature of our subject, it is difficult to utilize tangible evidence to illustrate it. Nevertheless, there are multiple provocative phenomena which support the hypothesis that "George" survives the death of the body and continues to function.

Let's continue down the list of subconscious functions and see how many apply after bodily death. We have dismissed the first three, swimming, giving birth, and hibernation, since the body is obviously necessary for these.

The next function on the list is memory. There are on record, in many ways, over many years, other peoples' experiences which have convinced them that certain knowledge of past events could have been obtained only from the memory of deceased people.

These memories have been communicated to the living in many ways—by direct visions of the departed, manifested usually in sleep, in which the departed were heard to speak, or were heard to speak without their visual appearances (clairaudience). They were communicated also by direct contact through automatic writing, the oija board, the planchette, etc., or indirectly through the use of intermediates called mediums or sensitives. The evidential material from such communication with the departed produced knowledge which no *living* entity knew; its only known source is the minds of the departed. For example, messages of accidental death have been received from a person who died, and this person was the only one who knew, at that particular time, that he had died.

Personal experiences are always the most convincing. One can hear about others' experiences and with a skeptical shrug easily dismiss them as coincidence, or fraud, or error. But let it happen to you personally, and how that complacency is shaken!

Mediumistic proof

Our first experiences leading us further to believe that one does survive bodily death came via the mediumship of Reverend Arthur Ford. Although we had heard of him before, having read his collaborated autobiography,[2] we knew he had never heard of us. We have always followed the motto "Never leave a stone unturned" so we decided to attend a convention of the Spiritual Frontiers Fellowship in Chicago a few years ago, having seen Reverend Ford's name on the program, to see whether we could arrange a "sitting" with him. Our practice of personally testing every medium or sensitive we possibly can was never more productive than at our initial sitting with Reverend Ford.

As described in his autobiography, he goes into a trance-like state and a "messenger" runs errands for him "on the other side." This messenger or guide is called "Fletcher" and is a deceased childhood friend of Arthur's.

After Reverend Ford achieved the sleep-like trance, Fletcher began presenting to us deceased relatives and friends of ours, forming a kind of "reunion." "Mina and Andy are here." "Mina just came over. She is so new, she needs the guide to help her." My mother's unusual name, Mina, was no problem to Fletcher. He knew, too, that she had died only a few months before in a home for the elderly in Kansas and was therefore a newcomer. How did he know this? "Andy has been with us a long time. He's so glad you were able to get through all your schooling without his help." My father, Andrew, died when I was a mere lad. "Mother Rose is here. She came over so young she looks like a bride." Dorothy's mother, named Rose, died when Dorothy was four years old. There followed pleasant remembrances of our lives together, little personal things.

Skeptics will argue that the medium is "merely" obtaining this information by telepathy from the minds of the living, not the dead. This, of course, could hardly apply to that incident which was in the mind of the deceased *only*. It could conceivably be an

---

[2] Margueritte Harmon Bro, *Nothing So Strange* (New York: Harper & Row, Publishers, Inc., 1958).

explanation for any material given which was in the minds of some living person.

To anyone present at the sitting, the rapidity and the unhesitatingly smooth nature of the delivery by the medium would suggest otherwise. Such presumed remarkable telepathic powers, capable of such super ability along telepathic lines, seems hardly likely. Even the most remarkable telepathists known would find difficulty in regularly performing such feats. The most likely explanation to us is the simpler one—that this material was coming from the surviving subconscious minds the "noncorporal personal agencies" of the deceased.

The "tape recorder" of subconscious memory does, then, seem to function after bodily death.

Telepathy as communication

Our next instinctual function (No. 5) is telepathy. Can the separated surviving subconscious mind telepathically perceive, just as it did when attached to the living body? The evidence suggests that it can perceive even better without those interfering clouds of the bodily conscious mind.

In the first session with Reverend Ford and his friend Fletcher, reassurance on a little personal problem was given, without being requested. At another session a few years later, I organized in my mind multiple questions I wished advice on, and sat silently as they were answered one by one by my "guide" (spiritual advisor) without my needing to utter a sound. How much convincing does it take to illustrate thought perception?

Telepathic ability between surviving subconscious minds is again and again reported to be the regular means of inter-communication in the astral world. Such reports from widely varying sources over many years all consistently demonstrate the lack of the need of verbal communication between surviving subconscious minds—they can all perceive the thought itself; it does not need to be otherwise expressed. With no bodily conscious mind to interfere, telepathy seems to become crystal clear and utilized regularly rather than spasmodically.

Clairvoyance and its aspects

The next function, clairvoyance (No. 6) or the ability to "see" objects via the subconscious "mind's eye" is, like telepathy, hard to separate from the same function in the living person. In other words, it is hard to isolate completely telepathic and clairvoyant powers of the perceiver from those of the perceived. In many a purported contact with the surviving spirits the entities' apparent ability to perceive the *physical set-up* is similarly manifested as their ability to perceive the *thoughts* of the participants.

A coach's widow coaches the team clairvoyantly

After giving lectures on this subject, I regularly ask for examples of personal experiences from my audiences. At a businessmen's luncheon, a distinguished gray-haired community leader furnished an excellent example illustrating apparent clairvoyant powers of the deceased. He had been on the boxing team in college years ago and the boxing coach had suddenly died of a heart attack. The school term had just started so it was impossible to get a replacement until the next year. The widow of the coach was a sensitive or medium and she received the message from her deceased husband to let him continue coaching the boxing matches for the rest of the year utilizing her mediumistic channels for communication.

Being rather desperate for coaching, the team did exactly this. The widow lay in a trance state in a distant dressing room and gave the round by round corrections and instructions from her husband during the matches. The instructions would point out details of the action in each round, such as "You're holding your left too low," etc., and were so accurate that the team won the championship that year.

Now, the widow's subconscious mind could have been clairvoyantly watching the match, but she knew nothing about boxing! She might have been telepathically reading some living person's subconscious mind, but whose would have been capable of such detailed coaching ability? Again, the simpler explanation would be more acceptable: the deceased coach was finishing out the school term.

I know of no way to exclude completely the power of the living person's subconscious mind from the powers of the non-living other than to accept the rule that the simpler explanation is the more likely.

If living subconscious minds were capable of such super

clairvoyance, it is odd that they do not manifest it more widely and more often rather than only on rare occasions such as seances, dreams, etc.

Precognition or prophecy

The next function, precognition or prophecy (No. 7), has been attributed to the spirit world for centuries. Visions, dreams, and voices from departed loved ones giving timely warning, *in advance,* of impending danger are being accumulated in a steadily increasing number by students of parapsychology. These are so numerous, so familiar, and emanate from so many sources that we will not dwell on them here.

The five senses in spirit communication

The next five (No's. 8, 9, 10, 11 and 12) represent the known senses of sight, hearing, touch, smell, and taste. Again, according to the evidence presented, purported to be derived from unattached "Georges" or non-corporeal personal agencies, these are said to function acutely.

Spirit communication shows no limit to these abilities. In fact, the variety of colors, fragrances, sounds, tastes, etc., experienced in the unobstructed universe of the astral world are very poetically described, and the "passed over" entity often expresses regret that his loved one, still obstructed by earthly life, cannot as yet share the beauty offered by these heightened senses with their far broader spectrum of perception.

Genetic Memory

Genetic memory, No. 13, is a carryover in the chromatin of genes from parent to progeny and as part of a physical or material transference, does not play a role in survival of bodily death.

Psychokinesis—its significance

Now we come to No. 14, psychokinesis. Can the subconscious minds of those who have departed earthly bodily life act upon physical objects and cause kinetic motion, physical action?

We are going to dwell on this particular instinctual function at greater length because it incorporates one of the theoretical explanations for the "things" that have happened at Bradmar. These physical happenings are loosely labeled "poltergeist" phenomena or "noisy ghosts." In explaining them there are two theoretical explanations to consider. The first, and in our minds least likely, is that these phenomena are produced by the psychokinetic action of the bored or mischievous subconscious minds, usually of living adolescent or preadolescent children. As any parent can testify, capriciousness of behavior is characteristic of this age group. They are in transition, neither adults nor children, but alternate between in their actions. The late Dr. Nandor Fodor has written extensively on this theory. Such an explanation seems apt on some occasions. It is suggested by the statistically high incidence of adolescent children living in houses where such manifestations occur. It is also suggested by the decreased incidence of phenomena (in a house where it occurs regularly) during the period when the children's attention is preoccupied, as in watching favorite programs on television. Even their capricious Georges enjoy cowboy western shows, statistics seem to indicate.

There is probably no one simple explanation for such phenomena.

However, the physical happenings that we have described in earlier chapters have been associated in our minds with definite purposes, definite meaningful events or ideas to such a degree that our reason balks at the concept that they were all just idle mischief. They seem in our case to be intelligence-directed, and of a higher level than pre-adolescent capriciousness.

The second theory, therefore, the one which seems more likely to us, is that these physical happenings were effected by deceased people manifesting via psychokinesis and utilizing this power for a purpose.

An example of such purposeful psychokinetic effect produced by a surviving subconscious mind would be the story of the split beam at Bradmar, referred to previously. The former owner and occupant of Bradmar had told many friends, neighbors, and relatives that when she died she wanted to be put in her coffin in front of the great fireplace; that she would that night cause the large beam to split in the ceiling directly overhead. This is exactly what happened; the beam split with a resounding "crack." We have heard this story from so many varying sources since purchasing the house that there seems little doubt about its accuracy.

Of course it is still "possible" that sheer coincidence could be involved, but this event joined with the steadily increasing list of paranormal phenomena occurring at Bradmar would make such an explanation, indeed, quite a coincidence.

It could "possibly" have occurred from psychokinetic activity of some living person's mind, but this seems unlikely as the woman had so repeatedly stated her plan of action before her death.

Another odd fact exists in relation to the split beam. The split is a series of angled cracks which peculiarly occur in the center portion of the wood for the full length of the long beam and do not "follow through" with the pattern of the grain to the edge, as one would logically expect. Such a series of small incomplete splits appears odd and, yet, also purposeful in that they do not really weaken the beam as a support.

No one knows why this particular phenomenon was chosen by the deceased, but we must assume that she had her own purpose.

Too, in our opinion, the other "things" that have happened to us directly were associated with some purpose rather than occurring at random.

To illustrate: That fateful Saturday afternoon when the ornamental grill on the planter was torn out of its moorings, when the waving leaf, the unexplained loud crash, and the first of the electric light phenomena occurred—was the day before the one on which I had arranged to present publically for the first time my views on spiritual and paranormal phenomena.

I personally felt that this activity was caused by interested entities in the spirit world who were thereby expressing their approval of my decision. This may be pure association rather than causation, but it was significant to us that such a shower of phenomena should immediately follow the decision to give public talks on this subject. The first lecture was received by so much public interest and enthusiasm that the number of lectures succeeding it is now well in the hundreds.

Pattern of paranormal occurrences

As time went by we began to recognize a pattern whereby paranormal occurrences seemed to be followed shortly by some significant change in our lives.

About one month before we found Bradmar, one of our two

bedroom lamps went on spontaneously three separate times and one went off spontaneously once. With the first occurrence the one on the right went on spontaneously at 3:00 A.M. waking us out of a sound sleep. A week later the one on the left went on at 12:30 A.M. Another week later while Dorothy was reading in bed, the one on the opposite side lit up. On that evening there was a distinct, repeated popping sound on the ceiling. Dorothy assumed that it was an insect bumping against the ceiling but thought it odd that it could make so much noise and yet not be large enough to be visible.

The following evening when I was again sitting up in bed reading, I was startled to have the lamp I was reading by go off suddenly, plunging the room into darkness. As I turned the light back on, the popping noise I had heard the night before became very loud and insistent. The sound was located on the ceiling, and just as I was wondering if there could be a mouse or something in the attic making such a peculiar noise, the sound jumped from the ceiling to a side wall. It was so localized that I got out of bed and pressed my ear against the wall. I could clearly hear this distinct tapping sound that seemed to be in the wall itself! It was an outer wall with no room opposite. It continued until I went to sleep without any cause being apparent.

After we had found Bradmar and while we were working to restore the house, we had a flurry of activity with lights going on at both houses. Two of these were the first to occur in daylight. One was an overhead light in Karl Vogel's room, while painting was being done; the other was at our former house in the evening while the sun was still shining.

The next spring there was another series of lights going on every morning at 4:30 A.M. for three consecutive mornings that preceded emotionally stressful situations of severe illness in our children.

A cousin and her small baby were visiting on another occasion. A light went on during the night by the baby's bed and within a few weeks the child became so seriously ill that a series of hospitalizations and surgery followed. The child recovered eventually.

There were no more light phenomena until about a year later when the bedroom light went on again in the mid-afternoon. Within twenty-four hours Sieg's father fell in the yard injuring himself, and we received two letters that were very disturbing.

Before long the family grew accustomed to expect something

to happen following these phenomena but always with a feeling of reassurance that it would turn out well. *We acquired confidence in these timely forewarnings that we were being watched over by those who cared for our welfare.* This has always been a comfortable and reassuring feeling which is shared by all members of the family. Never have our paranormal phenomena produced fear or anxiety in any one of us.

How psychokinesis informs and helps

The children have learned to rely on this feeling of an ever present source of help in time of need. For example—our eldest son had been struggling unsuccessfully with a large wrench trying to loosen a rusty connection on a 6-inch water irrigation pipe. Sieg's mother had died a few days before, and the lad couldn't get the large rusty connection to turn in spite of the enormous wrench he was using until he verbally appealed "O.K., Grandma, give us some help." His *acceptance* and practical utilization of the psychokinetic power of this source evidently paid off well, for, after the many previous unsuccessful pulls, on the next pull after asking for Grandmother's help it gave way and turned so readily that he was caught off balance and fell over on his back in the water!

Another year later the most dramatic of all the light phenomena occurred with no particular significant personal changes we could associate with it, as yet. This was at 12:30 A.M. the night of July 13th, and one of the bedroom lights acted up. We were awakened by the clicking on and off of the switch which is located on the headboard of the bed. The switch sounded as if it were going on and off several times, but without the lamp lighting up. Then the light started going on and off with the switch noise continuing, and we estimated twelve times on and twelve times off as we watched agape.

The lamp and its connections had functioned perfectly for years before. And it has worked well since, with no evidence of defects.

About a month later the same lamp went on in mid-afternoon, and four hours later we were without water because the pump system furnishing the house broke down completely.

Another physical phenomenon followed by an important event was the bobbing about of the large brass chandelier suspended by a long heavy chain in Bradmar's twenty-one foot high great hall. One of the children called, "Mama, come look at what the chandelier's doing!"

I came running as did three other members of the family. The large chandelier was bobbing about much like a bobber on a fishing line. My first thought was that we were having an earth tremor, but there was no motion felt on the stairs where we were standing. Also, a very delicate cut-crystal chandelier in the adjacent hall, although lighter in weight and seemingly more sensitive to tremors, was hanging perfectly still. Within two hours we received notice of the hospitalization and severe illness of another member of the family, again with a good recovery resulting.

Another reason for our belief that physical phenomena are more likely associated with the spirit world than living adolescent subconscious psychokinesis, is the example of the sounds of footsteps without anyone being visibly there. This was previously cited on two occasions with Karl Vogel's experience at Bradmar prior to our moving in. It occurred again, this time involving Mrs. Bradley and her sister Mary.

It was New Year's Eve and they had stayed up to talk and read after the remaining members of the family had retired, except for Karl who was out at a New Year's Eve party.

In the quiet of the house, Mrs. Bradley relates, I could hear someone walking through the carpeted area of the dining room hall. About the time I stopped reading to listen, the footsteps hit the hard marble of the floor in the great hall and they sounded so much like Karl's heavy leather heels that Mary spoke in surprise, "Is Karl home so early from a New Year's Eve party?" It was, after all, only 12:30 A.M. We listened in anticipation, expecting him to ascend the stairs and tell us about the party. However, after about five footsteps there was not another sound. I said to Mary that he must have decided to go back to the kitchen for a cup of coffee. She said, "What did he do, float?"

I, too, realized that, since the footsteps were so loud, we should have heard them receding to the kitchen. But there had been sudden silence. Further, I was aware that the few footsteps we had heard would not have sufficed to take him even a fourth of the distance to the coat closet. In curiosity I went from our bedroom into the adjacent sitting room which is built out from the main body of the house, and looked back at the entire house—there was not a light on except ours. It was then that I realized we had heard "non-corporeal personal agency" footsteps!

On checking with Karl the next morning, we learned that the party had indeed been very successful and he had not returned until 4:00 A.M.

Although it may be possible for mischievous subconscious minds of living adolescents to psychokinetically reproduce these sounds of footsteps, again, the simpler explanation for "Who Walks at Bradmar" would seem to be purposeful visits by surviving adults.

Do animals survive death?

There is controversial discussion regarding the survival of animals after death. Our family does not question this premise since further evidence of survival after death came from a rather unexpected source. One of our dogs was a tiny two-pound Chihuahua who when let outdoors in the winter, would shortly bark his piercing, shrill bark to be let back in. He hated the outdoors summer or winter and would make himself irritatingly obnoxious until let back in.

It was just before Christmas. The winter weather had set in. The family was busily making holiday preparations and on this night was involved primarily in trimming the tree. We hadn't noticed that the little dog had been let out (he had not barked to be let in) until one of the children noticed that he was missing.

A search for the dog was started immediately by the children, but to no avail. We all then joined in the search both indoors and out, because I had the definite feeling something was wrong with the dog. We systematically searched and called outside the house and, not finding him, began a systematic search inside.

Dorothy and Sieg remained at the Christmas tree, continuing to decorate. As the search party came to this hall where the tree was, Dorothy and Sieg were surprised to hear us all worriedly wondering where the dog could be. They assured us they had heard his series of shrill barks just before we came and supposed we had found him. We asked them, "Which direction did the barking sounds come from?" They both seemed confused and pointed vaguely up toward the center hall, somewhere. I immediately said, "He's dead. That was an astral bark you heard! He's met something unfamiliar and is giving his usual hostile reaction." I had the sudden conviction we would find him dead. I got a flashlight and carefully explored the dark corners outside the house, and sure enough, there he was, frozen to death, just outside the window within a few feet from where Sieg and Dorothy were working trimming the tree. Fifteen to twenty minutes before on our first search I had stood practically at that spot and tapped on that window to ask Sieg to turn on the outside lights. I must have been within inches of the dog at that time but he was in a shadow where I couldn't see him. However, he was of vivacious nature and had he then been alive would have made himself known.

Examination showed his tongue and throat to be frozen solid, his jaws frozen shut. How was it possible for Dorothy and Sieg to have heard his series of vivacious shrill barks just a few minutes before? And, why were the sounds they heard coming from the opposite direction and from "on high"?

Psychokinetic activity with particular objects

Another reason we feel that there is survival of death is the association of repeated psychokinetic activity with particular physical objects. These objects are usually familiar household items to which the deceased became emotionally attached during bodily life.

It is unlikely that capricious pre-adolescent subconscious minds would carefully follow around objects, like furniture, through various owners and over many years of time. Surviving spirits, on the contrary, are more likely to manifest such over-attachment to familiar physical objects for many, many years. True, such types of spirit would not be highly evolved. But repeated spirit messages show that bodily death does not, in itself, alter the level of evolvement of the mind. In other words, just because you die does not mean you immediately become angelic, all knowing, or wise.

An example in our experience of such attachment to physical objects came about when a lady called, having heard of our interest, seeking reassurance about the physical phenomena that had happened and was still happening in her home. She proceeded to tell us a fascinating story of having bought a house completely furnished that had formerly belonged to a widow and her elderly mother. It had been their home where they had resided many years. The two ladies had passed away leaving no heirs and the house had been purchased completely furnished including accessories and objets d'art.

After having moved, the new occupants were cleaning the

house. There were two small copper vases which appeared to need dusting. The woman took them to the bathroom toilet bowl and dumped out the contents, including two wads of cotton. On flushing the toilet she was frustrated when these cotton wads would not go down. Her frustration increased with repeated attempts. She finally gave up in desperation and later in the day while out in the yard visiting with a new neighbor, she idly retold the story. She was aghast when her neighbor told her that these two vases contained the ashes of the former owner's husband and father, respectively!

She had attributed the many years of subsequent happenings to their family to the indignities the deceased had suffered at her hands. These happenings followed them about on various moves to various states, and eventually to Denver.

On my second or third conversation with this lady, I learned that physical phenomena had become so disturbing to them that she had persuaded her husband to dispose of the vases and not even let her know how or where.

I was horrified that what might prove to be good reproducible evidence was so lightly tossed away. I prevailed on her to please ask her husband to retrieve them for us, let us have them, and she need not see or contact them again. He could send them to us in the mail.

Within three days the vases arrived in the mail, and I called to thank her for her trouble. I asked her whether she had found out from her husband where he had chosen to dispose of them. He told her that he had furtively deposited them in a large urn in one of the local cemeteries. Both became squeamish the next morning when they received a letter in the mail from this very same cemetery asking whether they would like to purchase a burial plot! They couldn't decide whether this was a coincidence—but were afraid to look into it further. We put the vases on the mantel in our bedroom, but nothing ever happened that could be attributed to them, much to our disappointment.

Poltergeist continues with other objects

I was not to talk to her again for many months. She then told me how the absence of the vases had not diminished the strange physical occurrences at her home. The same things were continuing—sounds of footsteps, rappings in the attic, lights going on, sounds of large animal growls, chairs skidding around in the kitchen, the eldest son's bed being violently shaken at night, sounds of beads spilling on the floor, and their good perfume being dumped out of the bottles.

She decided that the cause of these phenomena wasn't the vases after all but the old sleigh type bed which was part of the widow's personal bedroom suite. They had noticed that whenever this bed was set up, there was an associated increase in the phenomena. So she had decided to dispose of the bed. Again, we were horrified and prevailed upon her to tell us where she had sold it. She was very reluctant to tell us where it was, since she didn't want to be responsible for what might happen. She had felt it her duty to warn the antique dealer, but it was interesting to us that when we purchased the old sleigh-bed, he did not mention the warning.

What had made them decide to sell the bed was that on their move to Denver, she had decided to use the big old bed in spite of these associated phenomena, having been out the expense of transporting it. However, after it was set up there was an increase, again, in the phenomena. Again the sounds of the spilled beads, again the spilling of the perfume. The dresser kept coming out from the wall. The final "straw" was a violent Karate type of blow on the bed between her and her husband. This was followed by a strong force of some nature pulling her by the ankle as if to pull her off the bed. She needed her husband's counter-pull to remain on the bed! There are no adolescents in this home—the children are college level or married.

After we brought the sleigh-bed home and set it up, I was awakened out of sound sleep by the violent shaking of my own bed. The next night there was a loud "klunking" sound like that made by a man in heavy boots falling down the stairs, but no one was there.

Poltergeist always uninhibited

There are reported many cases of houses which continue to have paranormal phenomena in spite of successively different occupants. It seems more likely to trace the cause of these phenomena to non-corporeal personal agencies (surviving subconscious minds) who have emotional attachments to these structures and manifest them over many years—What is time to the departed?—than to assign the action to successive "crops" of adolescents.

We have gone down the list of instinctual functions and demonstrated how they tie in with evidence suggesting continuation of these powers after bodily death. Bear in mind the hypothesis that incarnation or association of these powers with a physical body does not enhance their function but, rather, that the body serves as an obstruction which in many ways interferes and blocks the action. The unattached, non-corporeal personal agency is unlimited, unobstructed, "free as a bird."

This does not mean that its powers cannot manifest while attached to the physical body. There are some individuals who spontaneously exhibit these functions, others who can utilize them at will, and all of us under the urgency of stressful situations manifest these inherent capabilities. They can also be elicited via deep meditation, via hypnotic trances, and via the currently popular consciousness expanding drugs (Psychedelics).

Dr. Nandor Fodor describes how Dr. Carl G. Jung "displayed his powers as a Poltergeist by making various articles in the room rattle on the furniture,"[3] on his first visit to Dr. Sigmund Freud.

---

[3] Nandor Fodor, *Between Two Worlds* (West Nyack, N.Y., Parker Publishing Co., Inc., 1965), p. 35.

Chapter 7

Reincarnation and
Life Before Birth

If the real "you" does not actually need the physical body to exist, if it can be separated during life and can continue to exist after bodily death, the thought may strike you that such an independent entity may have existed before it became attached to the earthly body. That perhaps this "you" was not created instantly at bodily birth as a shiny, new, blank blob, a previously non-existent, inexperienced "nothing."

I recall an illustration in the fly leaf of a psychology text I used in college. At the bottom of the page was a row of babies, appearing to be nearly identical, uniform little blobs of unmolded clay. In the upper margin were pictures showing how each one had been altered by the molding effect of experiences into very different, easily separable, adults. One was a crochety old maid; another a dignified, smartly dressed, successful figure; another a slovenly bum, etc.

Anyone working with new born babies would object to this implication. Workers in a newborn nursery will attest that babies are *not* all alike at birth! Of course there are minor physical differences from heredity but there are also behavioral patterns that cannot be attributed to heredity. They have individual personalities, individual traits, and are each as different in behavior patterns as are adults. Where did they get these traits?

Could it be possible that these little, pink new bodies house souls that are neither pink nor new but that are *sub*-conscious carry-overs entering a new phase of potential development by being attached to new conscious minds, the latter not yet developed, with literally a "new lease on life?"

Is it any more surprising and wondrous to be born again than to have been born once?

Evidence of separate life before birth

We have presented evidence that "you" continue to exist after the body is gone; is there evidence that "you" existed before the body began? Yes, there is evidence. Let's make the assumption, establish the hypothesis, then study the evidence and see how it fits.

The hypothesis is that the subconscious human mind is a partial manifestation of the total personal agent and that this agent has existed a long, long time (perhaps always) and has been incarnated (bodily attached) and re-incarnated many times before. It has also existed and become more highly evolved from periods of astral existence (without bodily attachment) between and before incarnations.

For clarity consult the diagram in Figure 1, The Total Personal Agent. Note that the present life is depicted as the uppermost slice of the total personal agent. This consists of an attached living body, denoted by the solid line, with its conscious human mind functioning now during earth life. *Note:* Current experiences go down into and affect the subconscious mind (of this life) as indicated by the arrows; Contents of the subconscious minds acquired during former lives also exert an influence on the subconscious of the current life. You are today a composite of all your yesterdays. Where you are going will depend to a certain extent on where you have been. What you are capable of now and in the future will be related to what you have accomplished in your past, not merely in the past of this current life but in the compound past of all your previous lives. The dividing lines in the diagram are not barriers; there is constant interchange of free communication as indicated by the arrows.

Now how do the evidences available fit the hypothesis? Let's consider the following:

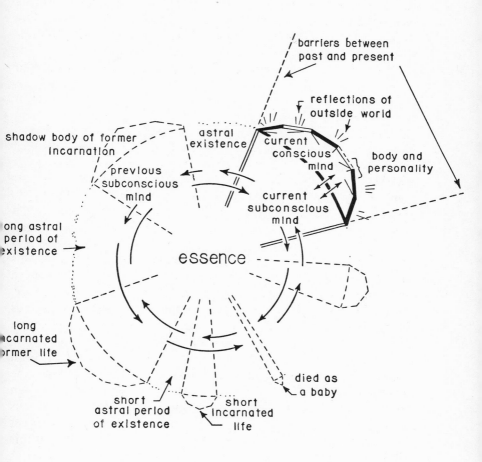

THE TOTAL PERSONAL AGENT

(The comprehensive all-inclusive real "you")

Figure 1

Child Prodigies—What makes them so?

How much better can one illustrate the compounding of development in multiple former lives than to point out the unusual abilities of individual children; abilities that existed in the child without prior teaching; instances of the pupil racing ahead of the teacher, actually knowing more than the teacher. Where did such knowledge come from?

There are mathematical geniuses capable of super-ability, even at tender ages. There are musical artists and composers who are obviously mature in their capabilities even while immature in their bodies. Mozart composed and played wondrous music at the age of five. Such ability cannot be explained by heredity or environment; it was there at birth.

Mentally retarded (conscious mind only?) children have been known to burst out with unexpected abilities under altered awareness, manifesting the contents of the undamaged and theoretically undamageable subconscious mind.

Here is another unexplored, potentially significant field for research. According to our hypothesis, the conscious mind *only* is capable of physical damage as it is part of the physical body. The subconscious, representing the total personal agent, is not dependent on the physical body and theoretically then could not be damaged by the obstetrical forceps, by the mother-medication, by the deprivation of oxygen from mother's anesthetics, or from inherited physical abnormalities.

Now if there is such severe conscious mind brain damage that no verbal communication has ever been acquired by the individual, then I do not see how we could demonstrate the underlying subconscious personal agent. However, there are thousands of mentally retarded children sitting idly in special homes who are not so severely retarded that they cannot speak, to some degree. Their attention spans are so impaired that the concentration necessary for deep hypnosis is usually not attainable; but what about the use of consciousness expanding psychedelic drugs? What a marvelous experiment could be done, utilizing these drugs and exploring their subconscious minds for evidences of previous lives, pre-existing knowledges and abilities. I have been told by speech therapists that the labored, difficult speech of spastic paralytics clears up and becomes sharp and unimpeded under hypnosis. There are multiple instances of spontaneous conscious break-throughs of mentally retarded individuals who manifest, temporarily, clear minds and unusual abilities. Let's put these psychedelic drugs to use in meaningful experiments.

The completed manuscript of this book had been sent to the publisher when the local newspaper, *The Denver Post*, featured in its Sunday, Nov. 7, 1965 edition, an article which we deemed so revealing, applicable, and significant that we are adding this insert here and quoting the article in its entirety:

Idiot Savant Twins Found Infallible For 2,000-7,000 Years[1]

By Murray Schumach

New York—"The first Wednesday in July of 1901 was on what date?" the doctor asked the mentally retarded 26-year-old twins at the New York Psychiatric Institute and Hospital.

"That was on the third," they replied correctly, almost instantly.

"If," the doctor then asked, "a box of candy cost 35 cents and I gave you a dollar, how much change would you get?"

The pale blue eyes of the identical twins blinked almost in unison behind thick glasses as they concentrated for several seconds.

"Fifty cents," said George, the quicker of the twins. His brother, Charles, echoed the answer.

Their questioner, Dr. William A. Horwitz, assistant direc-'tor of the institute, went briskly along with other questions, getting correct answers to almost impossible questions and incorrect ones to those that could be answered by any schoolboy.

For many years psychiatry has known of this rare type. The idiot savant is a mentally retarded person with some extraordinary mental gift. But George and Charles are, Dr. Horwitz says, the only known twins who are idiot savants. Originally they were triplets, but the sister died shortly after birth.

Experts all over the world study them and are confounded by them. Their intellectual achievements go far beyond trick memory of calendars. They seem to possess some complex mathematical ability, yet they cannot do the simplest multiplication or division.

When told a date on which a person died a few hundred years ago, they can respond at once. When asked how old that person would be if alive today, or when asked how they know that February 15, 2002 will be on a Friday or that April 21, 1968 will be a Sunday, as it had been in 1967, 1957 and 1946, they say simply that they do not know.

For half an hour, as Dr. Horwitz asked questions, they

proved his contention that George can answer, without error and instantly, all sorts of questions about dates covering 7,000 years beginning with the year 1. Charles is infallible for 2,000 years. They have an I.Q. of about 70.

In speech, they often sounded childish. Once, without warning, George said:

"They don't tease us here. We are happy here."

Dr. Horwitz asked them how long they wanted to remain. They replied together: "Until we are in heaven."

George has an uncanny memory for things other than dates. He can recall, in some detail, the weather for any day in the last five years. A reporter who suggested five dates in the last five years received such answers as:

"I remember that day. It was sunny in the morning and it rained in the evening. It was cool. In the thirties."

All the answers were correct and obviously based on his senses rather than what he read since he often gave details that were not contained in newspapers of that day.

Though there have been several theories about idiot savants, the prevailing one today is that the average person, if he or she concentrated on nothing but some particular memory skill would reach the same degree of efficiency in that field. However, the gifts of the twins at the institution seem to go beyond this explanation.

The last statement of the article could be labeled the understatement of the year! Yes, indeed, their gifts go far beyond such an inadequate explanation. Do take note how this material fits into our hypothesis: the concept of a damaged retarded conscious mind but the undamageable subconscious mind carrying over from previous lives; the super-memory of the current earth life unhampered by conscious overlay due to the undeveloped, child-like, and therefore non-interfering, conscious mind; the element of time manifesting either forward or backward; the fact that they don't know *how* they know these things, only *that* they do; that simple arithmetic, performed by the conscious mind, they are incapable of, but complicated calculation of the day of the week of a long distant or long past numerical date, they can tell you instantly. Note knowledge stretching back 7,000 years, unacquired in this life but already there at birth.

Note how the one twin named George (appropriately and coincidentally!) is sharper than his brother Charles and that his memory goes back 7,000 years whereas Charles' memory only goes back 2,000 years! Identical twin bodies do not hold identical twin souls, one is much older and, therefore, more capable. Does this fit into the hypothesis of reincarnation? Yes, by all means!

Note, with sorrow, the statement, "For many years psychiatry has known of this rare type." What have they been doing with this knowledge?

Parapsychologists, academicians, religious researchers—stop wondering aimlessly in your forests of verbalistic doubletalk; take these children into your laboratories. Age-regress them under careful psychedelic drug or hypnotic trances and study their total life story. Put the cards and dice away; such experiments were significant in their day but that was kindergarten. Excelsior!

Individuality at birth is independent of parents

If Edgar Cayce were alive today, I would encourage all my patients to have "life readings" done by him on all their children shortly after birth. Mr. Cayce could alter his conscious awareness until it included nearly (if not actually) total awareness. This marvelous man whose life is described in Thomas Sugrue's book *There is a River*[2] was capable of mentally functioning in self-imposed hypnotic trance on a level that incorporated his total life experience. He could also become aware of other people's total life experience and communicate this knowledge verbally.

Referring back to the diagram (Figure 1) of the total personal agent, note the multiple arrows in both directions connecting together the "spokes," the subconscious levels of all former existences. There is absolutely unlimited communication between the various "spokes" of this wheel of life. The conscious mind which is located external to the rim is actually out of the wheel, and communication of the contents of the wheel across this rim to the conscious mind is very difficult to achieve willfully and is far from "free."

Edgar Cayce could not *consciously* cross this rim but he was able to communicate across it by altering his conscious awareness in a self-imposed hypnotic trance, thereby becoming aware of his current subconscious mind, which in turn, was aware of his total personal agent experience, all of his former lives.

Now, recalling that telepathy and clairvoyance are perceptual instincts that function on a subconscious level, Edgar Cayce could also perceive the subconscious minds of others, as well as his own. This ability was pointed out by Gina Cerminara in her book *Many*

---

[2] Thomas Sugrue, *There is a River* (New York: Holt, Rhinehart and Winston & Inc., 1940, revised 1945).

Mansions in which she discusses Edgar Cayce. "The unconscious mind, moreover, is more easily accessible to other unconscious minds than is the conscious mind—it is generally easier to travel between two points in New York City by subway than by surface travel."[3]

I think this comparison is excellent. The conscious mind is so cluttered with everyday living necessities (income tax, mother-in-laws, competitive pursuit of the almighty dollar, etc.) that transportation is difficult. The "subway" of the subconscious is direct, fast, and efficient.

Why would I want a life-reading on all babies? In order that their paths through their current incarnation could be guided along routes appropriate to former lives. In order that we do not try to force square pegs into round holes, or vice versa.

The entire personality of the individual person is a reflection, subtle or otherwise, of his previous lives and experiences. If parents were cognizant of the previous patterns, they would not try to force their children into the parents' preconceived mold (often unconsciously based on their own deficiencies and disappointments) but would see the wisdom of letting their children follow their own predilections. The old adage for parents in relation to their children, "Have 'em, love 'em, and leave 'em be," seems to be the most difficult to follow in its last portion.

Child prodigies represent the most unusual and obvious carry-over of extra talent and are relatively few in number. But *all* children have behavioral patterns that represent carry-overs from past lives and, even if they are siblings living in the same environment, they are as different, personality wise, as different can be. If the parents are unaware of this carry-over and persist in clinging to the old concept that children are mere malleable blobs, they will do their utmost to mold their children to their own preconceived concepts—and are doomed to failure and heartbreak. Children just can't fit into their parents' behavioral molds because they were already "formed" when born.

This was well illustrated in an article by a psychologist who was the usual parent-critic until she became a parent: ("Good mothers, Impossible children—A Psychologist's View of what went wrong with all the theories, Edd J. Lesham, *Redbook* Magazine, April, 1965).

---

[3] Gina Cerminara, *Many Mansions* (Wm. Sloan Association, Inc., 1950), p. 44.

Children's individualities not molded by parents

This mother awakened to the fact that regardless of the parents, children seem to have built-in individualism not molded by attentive parents but existing in spite of, rather than due to, parents. The children of ministers, psychologists, etc., in the "just right" parental environment turn out to be shy, bold, social, anti-social, etc., regardless of their environments. Brothers and sisters may have an unchangeable like or dislike for each other manifested from birth and all the psychoanalyst's suggestions will go for naught. In fact they may jolly well be the psychoanalyst's own children!

Why can't those children be altered and molded nearer to the parents' heart's desire? Could it be because each has a pre-existing, set personality which is a carry-over from former lives? Because the child's total personality manifesting via his or her subconscious mind in this life reflects years and years of development in former lives and simply is not to be so easily altered by parents' whims in *this* relatively short life?

Many parents go about with their heads bowed in self condemnation over their children's choice of life work when, the truth is, they really had nothing to say or do about it in the first place. Have 'em, love 'em, and leave 'em be! They have the right to be themselves, just as you do. "Please, mother, I'd rather do it myself!" is the frantic plea of children to be allowed self development.

Now this does not mean absolute permissiveness in all things, Heaven forbid! They must be disciplined to proper behavior in the framework of society. We are referring to their basic personalities and their choice of goals in life—let them follow their own inclinations.

Of course, you as a parent must serve as a symbol of honesty, wholesomeness, and righteousness or regardless of their chosen life work, they may become mis-fits in any group.

Individuality, then, is present at birth and is a complex, complicated carry-over of former lives manifesting influence on the present life via the pathway of the subconscious. This may become handicapping, as evidenced by emotional conflict, with development of stomach ulcers when the round peg is trying to fit into the square hole, or may lead to a serene and creative life of adjustment reflecting a proper continuation of development channels in former lives. An example of the need for such adjustment would be the telephone operator who was informed by Edgar Cayce that she should be a commercial artist since she had made great progress in this field in former lives. She took his advice and utilized her previously unrecognized "natural talent" to rise rapidly in this field to great prominence. A round peg now fitting smoothly into a round hole.

Edgar Cayce and his influence

Although this book is primarily based upon our personal experiences at Bradmar, one cannot mention evidence of life before birth without paying due respect to the memory of this marvelous man whose recent life on earth was such a shining example of the proper utilization of former lives to aid his fellow man. As a medical doctor I blush with shame for my profession over the pitiful way he was misused and literally abused by my predecessors. In this respect he stands in noble company, for the history of medicine is replete with the persecution of pioneers and innovators by contemporaries and their eventual recognition and respect by subsequent generations. Were it not for the courage and perseverance of non-conformers, we modern doctors would still be treating all human illnesses by the application of leeches.

Progress cannot wait for acceptance by the common herd. Tradition breakers must pay the penalty of persecution. As stated in *Look* magazine of July 27, 1965, "The Battle of the Bible," page 19, "The Cross was not a Favorite Citizen Award handed to Jesus by the Jerusalem Chamber of Commerce...."

For the unfamiliar, Edgar Cayce lived at Virginia Beach, Virginia, and passed away on January 3, 1945, at the age of sixty-seven. During his productive life he treated successfully many human illnesses utilizing a profound knowledge of medicine and drugs that could not have been acquired in this life. It had to come from some other source, and the most logical explanation is simply that in his self-induced altered state of consciousness he was tapping the pool of knowledge acquired from former lives. Being an "old soul" who had led many lives, his pool was deep and rich with knowledge and perceptual abilities that gave great insight, not only into his own lives but into those of others. Anyone interested in pursuing his many contributions should contact the Association for Research and Enlightenment, Virginia Beach, Virginia.

Any explanations for Edgar Cayce's complete and detailed knowledge of medicine and pharmacy, as manifested in his self-induced trances, other than that this knowledge was a carry-over from former lives, would seem unreasonable. There just isn't any other suitable explanation. Mr. Cayce was also very capable of separating his subconscious mind from his body—sending it on errands apparently at will. Although, as we have discussed previously, all subconscious minds are separable from attached bodies, practice seems to help, and not just in playing the piano. It seems that he had died a long, horrible desert death in a previous life and had learned at that time to separate his subconscious mind from the body—it feels better! Remember "you" don't feel pain unless there is bodily attachment.

Hypnotic Age-Regression

The details of medical hypnosis are being saved for a subsequent chapter but, again, we must use evidence produced by hypnotic age-regression here, and go into detail on hypnosis, per se, later.

If our hypothesis holds true, that the human subconscious of this life is super-perceptual in many ways, can it also perceive its own former lives? If hypnosis is consciousness of the subconscious and memory is a part of the subconscious, can we, by suggestion, play back the "tape recorder" of memory of former lives utilizing the altered awareness of a hypnotic trance?

Any citizen of Pueblo, Colorado who is a friend of a businessman named Morey Bernstein would immediately say "sure!" and would begin to talk excitedly about a girl named Bridey Murphey.

Morey Bernstein is an amateur hypnotist and, I'm convinced, a good one and an honest one. I again blush with shame that age-regression under hypnosis seems to fall more in the province of businessmen's hobbies than in the ivied halls of academic scientists. I hope the future will alter this.

Mr. Bernstein was not the first, nor will he be the last, hypnotist to find, inadvertently or otherwise, that in hypnotic age-regression, awareness and memory do not begin suddenly with a "blurp" at the moment of birth as if the mechanism had just been snapped "on." Nor do they begin, as one might think, superficially, with the individual's acquiring language ability. Instead, one is impressed that the steadily flowing recall of past events continues smoothly beyond the age of the individual's knowledge of language, and beyond birth into the intrauterine life, *without diminution.* It is surprising how the subconscious mind finds nothing unusual in hearing and understanding the spoken word, before language was learned on the conscious level!

In exploring for "blips" or conscious-subconscious conflicts in the office practice of medical-hypnosis, it has become a regular procedure for me to regress to the intrauterine existence to see if the individual felt wanted—before birth. Many subjects emotionally describe how they heard their parent or parents express a desire for the opposite sex, prior to birth, and sob out "They didn't want me," revealing a subconscious feeling of rejection.

I have noted that if I ask any patient an illogical question, or make an impossible request, or give confusing suggestions, they will immediately come out of trance, open their eyes and consciously express the impossibility of what is wanted. However, in routine age-regression, going back in time and reliving past events, I feel it is very significant that not one ever opened his eyes and protested "But I am too young to understand talk." The subconscious mind hears, understands, and reacts to language before the conscious mind has learned it.

I wish all parents would verbally express happiness over expecting a *baby,* rather than specifying a boy or a girl.

I'll never forget the occasion when I became brave and first age-regressed a hypnotized patient beyond birth. This particular teenage young lady was quite hypnoidal, a very good subject, and I had steadily guided her back in time, having her relive her current life along selected paths of study: sibling relationships, peer relationships, parent relationships, etc. She was shy and demure in character and very respectful in her manner of answering my questions. I could tell by her emotional reactions, delayed answering time, etc., that she was in a medium to deep trance and had slowly retraced her life, further and further back. She recalled and relived with humor the time when she was six months old and her two-year-old sister had cut her baby hair with a pair of scissors—for which Mama administered said sister a spanking. We then regressed to Mama's "tummy" before she was born. She remarked about the cosy warmth and pleasant darkness and seemed very content until I asked her what she heard while there. She became very emotionally upset and began crying because neither her Mama nor her Daddy wanted her. I asked how she knew this and she wailed "because they wanted a boy and *I'm a girl!*"

After this emotional outburst had quieted down, I "took a deep breath" and stated, "You are now going back, back in time before you were in your Mama's tummy." I paused, then asked bluntly, "What's your name?"

If she had come out of trance, opened her eyes, looked at me and said, "What are *you,* some kind of nut?" I would not have been at all surprised.

But she didn't!

There was a long pause and then she blurted out, in an aggressive curt manner that was totally out of her character, "Marta!" This was not the name on her chart before me, and a tingle of excitement came over me. I gently asked, "Your last name?" She rudely tossed back "Swanson." This was not the name on the chart either. I asked "Where do you live?" She answered, "In the country." I asked, "What country?" and got back an impatient, "Norway, of course!" in a surly impudent tone of voice that implied any fool would know what country we're in.

Prior to this her personality had been shy, nearly demure, and very quietly respectful. This rough rudeness was entirely out of her present life character.

I asked, "What is the name of the nearest town?" "Oslo." "Your Father's name?" "Olof Swanson." "Your mother's name?" "Hilda." "How old are you?" "Sixteen." "Do you go to school?" "Yes." "What is the name of your school?" "I don't know." "What is the date on the calendar?" "I don't know."

And here she became very disturbed, breathed heavily and began to weep. "Do you go to church?" "Yes." "What does it look like?" "Very old, covered with vines, cracks in the wall. It has old pews where you kneel." "How do you get to the church?" "We ride our bicycles. It is beautiful." "You're now seventeen years old; what do you see?" "My Mama's crying because I'm gone." "Where did you go?" "To nowhere, my Mama's crying." Here she became very upset over her mother, her breathing was rapid and she began to cry. "Did you die?" "Yes." "Where?" "At home. I was sick, in my bed." "How old are you?" "I was sixteen, I hurt, I was sick." She became upset again. "You've already died. Did you see your funeral?" "Yes." "Who came?" "My friends. My Mama's crying." Again upset as she talks about her Mama. "Did your Papa cry?" Indignantly, "No, he's a very strong man, he's so big." "After you died, where are you?" "I was nowhere."

"Then what happened?" "It was dark. I was warm." "What made you warm?" "My mother."

We then repeated the birth and the experience of warm to cold, dark to light, etc., that was identical to the age-regressed experience in this life.

I had run out of office time and after discussing it with her husband asked the young lady to join us at a later date at our residence with the family.

In office treatment utilizing hypnosis, the purpose is to get the patients to understand themselves better so that I have not suggested amnesia but rather, the opposite, that they "will remember everything."

I was, therefore, curious as to what reaction the patient herself would have to this material she manifested before birth. I didn't get a chance to ask, for upon awakening she immediately and spontaneously asked, "I didn't know you would lie under hypnosis?" I said, "Why did you ask? Did you lie to me?" She answered increduously, "Well you certainly didn't believe all that crazy stuff, did you?"

She had never heard of re-incarnation, vaguely knew the name Bridey Murphey but had neither read the book nor seen the movie. It was very obvious that she didn't entertain any prior knowledge of the concepts of life before birth and thought the present business was "a pack of lies." I pinned her down, "Why did you lie to me?" She looked confused and answered in bewilderment and honestly, "I don't know."

I had not been prepared for a study session in the office, and wouldn't have had the time had I been prepared. I had acted on an impulse because of the good trance ability of the patient. We arranged a more careful session at our home later to be tape recorded.

As several months had elapsed, I could not remember the details of the first session and had to consult what I had written on her chart. However, as it turned out "Marta" not only remembered and repeated accurately the identical information but also could not be tricked into varying her "pack of lies."

After getting our young lady settled comfortably on the sofa, I rapidly repeated the hypnotic induction technique then jumped back to an emotional event that occurred when she was two years old (her "doggie was killed by a car"), taking my cue from the previous session. We then repeated the regression to beyond birth and got the identical responses as to name, place, parents, etc. I led Marta through childhood to gradually older ages thinking I would trick her beyond the point where she had died according to the previous session.

It didn't work. At age sixteen, as we were going ahead in time, she interrupted a question about some triviality, got a pained suffering look on her face, began breathing rapidly and more rapidly, loosened the collar on her dress, began fanning herself with her hand, and rather piteously kept repeating, "I'm so hot. It's so hot, etc." I asked, "What's the matter?" She said weakly, "I'm sick. I'm so sick." "What is your mother doing now?" "She's washing me with a cold cloth." "What is your father doing?" "He's gone." "Where did he go?" "To get the doctor." "Did the doctor come?" "No." She then started shivering and wrapped her arms about herself, teeth chattering, "I'm so cold." "What is your mother doing now?" "She's putting blankets on me." "Did your Daddy come back?" "No." She had been breathing more and more heavily and labored in style. She was thrashing around, tossing and turning. Now, suddenly, she stopped moving, apparently stopped breathing and lay deathly still. Her moaning ceased. A girl friend who had accompanied her to this session this evening was frightened and later told us, "Gosh, I thought she *had* died!"

There was a long silence. I asked, "What are you doing now?" She answered, "Nothing." "Where are you?" "I'm dead." "What is your mother doing now?" "Crying." "Did your father get back with the doctor?" "No." There followed a series of questions which covered her funeral and her friends who sat in the front row with her parents as she had no brothers or sisters. I asked again if her father cried and she very emphatically and disdainfully asserted, "My Daddy doesn't cry. He's a man!" "Where are you?" "Nowhere." "What are you wearing?" "Nothing." "Are you hungry?" "No, I don't eat." "What do you see?" "Nothing."

Awareness of incarnations

It is interesting here to note that these answers follow a similar pattern about the nature of the awareness between incarnations. If she were "lying," as she still consciously thinks, this would have been a convenient place to pad this up with her own or a biblical version of "heaven."

Other similar cases, including the famed Bridey Murphey case, give very little evidence of awareness in the astral existence between earthly lives. I have reason to doubt whether our subject was informed on this particular aspect. If she were "lying," it would have been evident here; therefore, this had significance. Apparently awareness of previous earthly life details is transmitted to the current subconscious and then to verbalization much more readily than non-earthly unattached experiences.

Even though I doubted that the trance was deep enough, I decided to make an attempt to get evidential material in the form of a knowledge of foreign language. I asked her at one point if she could tell us something in Norwegian. She paused a long time; then, as I had about given up, burst out with a sprightly little nursery rhyme which she rattled off rapidly. It sounded like a mixture of Norwegian and English and even though we couldn't understand it, we had her repeat it later and it sounded identical to our ears. She could remember it and repeat it unhesitatingly at a subconscious level in trance—and we onlookers functioning on a conscious level could not remember it even a few minutes later. Again, although I had not specified either way, she remembered after awakening the same things she had recalled in our previous session, but, significantly, did not recall at all the nursery rhyme.

Because her previous trance was apparently too light to know the date, we pinned her down with a direct question of the date on the calendar the day she died. After a long pause she came up with October 7, 1928. She was born in this life in 1943. We hope to get more details of the location of the farm where she lived as Marta in Norway and check on birth and death certificates.

Her long pause at our request for Norwegian speech represented a self-deepening of trance which carried spontaneous amnesia with it.

This encourages us to try, later, to spend much more time in deepening techniques to further eliminate the conscious mind and even the current subconscious to achieve true revivification, including methods of expression in character for that particular time. Similar studies have been reported many times by other workers. Now we need to convince the conscious mind of our subject of the importance of our work. At the present time I'm afraid she is still looking at us a bit askance for taking so much interest in her "pack of lies."

Let's refer back to our earlier discussion of the efficient tape recorder of memory contained in and utilized by the subconscious mind. Here was a beautiful illustration of the different memory abilities of the conscious compared to the subconscious mind. All of us on a conscious level had difficulty remembering the little, rhyming, two-line nursery rhyme. This included the subject who listened to herself recite the poem on our tape machine after she was conscious and the session over. A few minutes later I asked her to repeat it—still on a conscious level—and like the rest of us, she couldn't remember it. However, on a subconscious trance level she repeated it without hesitation when requested. *Note:* Conscious awareness interferes with memory—among many other things.

Our personal experience with age-regression beyond birth is amateurish and necessarily limited. Here again is a crying need for academic investigation. Psychedelic drugs have inadvertently brought out evidence of knowledge not acquired in the current life of the subject. Careful aiming towards a target of evidence of previous lives while under the influence of these new drugs, under careful academic planning and management, needs to be done.

Dr. Ian Stevenson, neurologist at the University of Virginia, has acted as an investigator on many cases of reported re-incarnation. Anyone interested in pursuing this field should check his investigations as reported.

The illogic of one life—the logic of many

Material energy is neither created nor destroyed. Even the tiniest particle does not disappear without a trace but is transformed, and continues to exist in another form. It seems illogical then that the creator of such a pattern with insignificant particles of matter would not similarly apply it to the most magnificent of all his creations, the soul, the total personal agent.

It also seems illogical that the struggle of life should have been futile, that intellectual achievements and spiritual development acquired through great effort should all go for naught.

It does seem logical that the lessons learned, the mistakes made, and the heights achieved in this life are but a part of a greater development towards ultimate wisdom and purification of the soul. There is a biological evolution from simpler to more complex structure in plants and animals, from the lower to the higher forms. It takes many lives, many generations to achieve these higher forms. It seems logical that spiritual development, similarly, is not just a one life affair. All of nature knows no extinction, only transformation. In considering the possibility that there is only one life—this is it, you have no other chance—there comes to mind the disturbing thought that the creator is infinitely cruel. If this is the *only* life, why does He favor some with gifts of good health, wealth, and all "the breaks" and assign to others deformed bodies, ill health, misfortune and catastrophe?

Conversely, if this life is but one of many lives, then such starting handicaps may not represent an imbalance of favors but rather a carry-over of previous problems with the chance, the privilege, to balance the scale of rights and wrongs.

If what we are, where we are, and what we have are but the results of yesterday's earnings, perhaps it would behoove us to stop long enough today to take stock of ourselves and the situation we find ourselves in, while there is still time to prepare for tomorrow.

It matters not whether we are satisfied or dissatisfied with what we see of today; today is set, it cannot be changed. The only constructive thing we can do with today is make the most of it, do the best we can and make a firm resolution as to what we want our future to be.

What a beautiful promise re-incarnation can be. How knowledge of this promise could change mankind, to know that no good deed done, no effort made is ever lost or wasted! One is almost staggered by the possibility that if this were universally known and accepted, these very principles would put an end to envy, jealousy, bitterness and a host of other ignoble emotions.

The gifts or deprivations resulting from the earnings of efforts of times past are referred to in some religions as *Karma*. I think no man should give blind adherence to any teaching that is not commended by reason and, for us, this teaching is the only one that gives logical answers to questions that have been asked for centuries.

There is probably for most people some traumatic event in their lives that they can look back on later and recognize as having been a turning point for them. A time when the pat answers of most dogmas and creeds no longer suffice because somehow they aren't answers; they don't serve to still the racing heart, full of fear and terror.

I remember well the day my turning point came. I was working as a bookkeeper for a group of doctors in St. Paul, Minnesota. The three of us who were in the office were busily working away as usual, and about us was the usual humdrum of the average day which was suddenly shattered for everyone by the exploding cries of a woman. All work came to an abrupt halt. No one made a move or uttered a sound, and I knew as I looked at the others that they felt the same cold, clutching fear I felt. For this was no ordinary cry. This was a screaming protest to God, a begging, a groveling. When the first waves of the shock had passed, I got up from my desk and went to the door that led into one of the pediatricians' offices. I could make out by the conversation, that he had just told them their beautiful little girl had leukemia and wouldn't live out the year. The doctor continued talking in a low and even tone, but it seemed to me that the look of quiet tragedy on the face of the father was only intensified as the doctor kept referring to this as "The will of God."

It seemed small wonder to me that it was little consolation to this father to slough off this tragedy as "The will of God." For here was I, having no connection with this scene at all, and yet I was flooded with the feeling of outrage toward the God that should let this happen. What outrageous thing had this little child done that it should be the "Will of God" that she be snatched out of the arms of parents who adored her. How was I to know, if such a God existed, that he wouldn't also decide on some whim to take my baby. I was at this time four months pregnant with my first baby, a baby I had waited nine years for. I had already lost six. And now for the first time I had been able to keep one long enough to feel movement. And no one but another mother will know the excitement and the miracle of that!

As I stood there in the doorway, I became faint with fear that this was all just a joke. What if He, this God, were just going to let me have this baby long enough to see it, know it and love it and then take it away from me! What sort of a God is this! It can't be! But from that day on, I started looking for better answers than my church had given me up to this point.

The first insight I had into the possibility of such a thing as Karma came when I remembered something from the Bible. I remembered that one of the disciples said to Jesus, "Master, who did sin? This man, or his parents that he was born blind?" And without then understanding the full implication of this, it still somehow brought solace to my still aching heart.

The years have passed and I now have three beautiful and healthy sons and, believe me, none of them is a joke. But during these years I have read and dug and delved and asked and looked and thought and pondered and read some more.

Lots of answers I found. Some weren't entirely satisfactory, some only called for more answers, but this can be good. One of the first things I came across was, "When the desire rises, a soul takes its first step." I'd hoped there weren't any restrictions on this. I hoped it meant a desire for truth with a resulting right to question, and a right to have answers that didn't insult my intelligence.

Answers as received from many sources

The answers I finally came to be satisfied with have come my way from a thousand different sources. All the way from the Bible to the Eastern religions, to what is known today as mediums. Is there anyone left who doesn't know of the wonderful work done by Edgar Cayce or Arthur Ford, while in trance?

One of the most pressing questions to me was: if a man sins unknowingly and perhaps hurts one or many as a consequence of his sin, is he held as responsible as if he had a black heart and a forked tail? Would this still be his sin to work out?

I don't know why I was particularly concerned with this, I don't remember having a guilty conscience over anything special at the time. Perhaps it was just a longing, left over from the experience in the doctor's office, a longing to know that there was a built-in, guaranteed justice with no favorites.

From the answers I have received , would seem that the laws of Heaven are more liberal than civil law is. Civil law states that "Ignorance of the Law is no excuse." But when it comes to offending God, it's what's in the heart that matters, the "Intention," and, none are punished for error they were unable to avoid. Here, of course, there is the great danger of alibing to oneself: That should be scrupulously avoided.

If a sin has indeed been committed, it is sheer folly to think you can fall on your knees in prayer and expect all the laws of the Universe to be changed to get you out of it. Woe to him who is counting on some magical incantation on his deathbed to wipe the slate clean and transform a hardened sinner into a radiant, shining saint.

The law of Karma should be looked upon as an opportunity

to right all wrongs done to self and fellow man, as a second chance, a million times over. Even more important than righting wrongs, is the opportunity hereby given for the soul's expansion, growth and purification. Your own individual opportunity to leaven the whole. What a thrilling concept that alone can be!

The question has been asked, "In view of these teachings of Karma, why should I then give to charity, or in any way hold out my hand to my fellow man, if I can assume that the plight he is in is of his own making?" What an easy way this would be to rationalize indifference. What a pitfall this could become. The truth is that one person's suffering cannot be isolated, but becomes another's opportunity to learn and rise above himself and therefore becomes a lesson for both. One person's suffering cannot be cut off, it does not exist in a vacuum. It has threads permeating all of creation. Thus we should bear one another's burdens.

When we accept the suffering of another and attempt to alleviate it, we lighten his Karma by teaching him the lesson of charity and by the same act confirm our own. We humbly rise and expand and so help make amends in the universe for mistakes made by others. This does not lessen the responsibility of the doer of the evil act, but helps him learn his lesson more quickly—if we can accept a pretty safe assumption: that it is better to teach by example, rather than punishment. By lending the helping hand, you strengthen your own spiritual muscles; it helps you to climb higher the mountain of spiritual perfection that some time or another, one way or another, must ultimately be climbed.

It is simply because this mountain must be climbed, that we come back again and again. One incarnation is always a preparation for the next. There is no marked cut. The whole of life flows on majestically and whatever flows into it from whatever source, that addition remains. If it is muddy water it must be purified; if it is pure water, it helps to clarify impurities that may be added later. The usual pattern is one of gradual learning, gradual strengthening of character, gradual growth in integrity, in charity and courage.

It takes many lives to cut a gem of many facets. The manifold facets cut during the course of time are what accounts for the beauty of the light that some souls seem to radiate. With each new life new brilliance is given the spirit, new insights are won, and new values added.

Balance as the most important element

Balance is the important element and the most difficult to maintain. With every new experience, every new thought, every new acquaintance or new book, the balance must be re-adjusted—just as the tightrope walker must adjust his balance to every breeze and every motion of the rope. For if we let all the buffeting of life's tempests throw us off balance, we lose ground and must repeat our steps, climb back upon our perch, shaken and bruised. Some time is then of course lost, and we are in danger of becoming discouraged and bitter. It sometimes takes a great deal of willpower and positive thinking to overcome such setbacks.

One should try to remember in times like this to fight, to put forth his greatest efforts, for ground gained under hardship always serves to encourage the weaker ones to try a little harder, hold on a little longer.

I have heard the question asked: "Is it necessary to suffer in order to grow in spiritual strength and stature?" The wisest answer I heard is, that it is not necessary to suffer in order to grow, but that no growth is possible without overcoming obstacles and meeting challenges. If life does not give them to you, you must find them. A truly advanced soul will bless his obstacles by treating them simply as challenges to be overcome, and make something good and beautiful from them. Jesus said "By their fruits you shall know them."

To know what you think and why you think it, is the best insurance you can have to peace of mind. Probably because I am a woman, I like the idea of making a house of your thoughts, carefully planning the architecture, making the whole structure solid and sound, so that it will stand up under attack and weathering. Come back to your house often, keeping it beautifully clean and well arranged. Keep it open to sunlight and the fresh air of new ideas and concepts. We will be great only if we think greatly. We will accomplish great things only if we think in terms of great dimensions.

The value of accomplishment

Accomplishment is essentially self-expression, and to express ourselves wholly and efficiently there must be great pressure from within our souls. We are dependent in our expression on the openness and force with which we go about it. If we have great drive but are tight in our attitude, we cannot express ourselves. If we are open but have little drive, we have no results either. Both the willingness and the effort to expend the energy to bring forth a result are needed for accomplishment. The goal must sink into the subconscious. It must fill the whole being. Extremes in anything are to be avoided and this is no exception. Some people struggle so to think in great dimensions, and make such an effort in striving for accomplishment, that they nearly strangle themselves in the process.

Our family has an acquaintance who drops by regularly, one of those people who always fits into whatever is going on and whose appearance is welcomed because of her own valuable contribution to the conversation. She has, however, one problem; she is always being troubled by guilt feelings if things start going exceptionally well for her, or she has purchased something that she didn't really have to have, but bought only because she couldn't resist its beauty. She tends to be very harsh on people whose only sin is that they have a very healthy and robust bank account. She is quick to condemn them as useless people who have frittered away their lives in spite of the fact they have contributed heavily, have in some cases been the sole backers for boys' schools, camps for orphans, nursing homes, churches and the local symphony.

It also happens that she thinks nature is the only valid voice of God. In case you haven't already guessed, she was reared by parents who were very good people but tended toward the narrow minded, hard core, bigoted traditionalists. When the lines are drawn I always find myself standing on the other side. But as the ensuing battles are always so stimulating, I don't really mind too much being at odds with her.

It is a running joke at our house about what a nature girl I am. To me one rock looks pretty much like another (if you've seen one, you've seen them all!) and all waterfalls are wet and noisy. I feel very much like the late Bob Benchley who never liked to go out-of-doors because he was afraid of getting hit by a meteorite.

I can quite accept the fact that my friend sees God in the rocks and hills and trees. I just refuse to believe that He has made this his only mode of expression. I like the thought that God is in everything. To me the miracle of it all is only compounded in a man-made thing of beauty.

When man, who is one of the ultimate creations of God, uses his talents which are both given and worked for by the individual soul, combines them with one of God's gifts of nature to produce a beautiful carving, a lovely table or a breathtaking painting, for me his work is an idealistic throught that has grown and become monumental.

My friend will agree with us that this is indeed art and a great creation. Then she will say "But it's not right to possess these things for yourself. They should be in museums." Museums there certainly should be, but I am convinced that if more people would make a conscious effort to weed out the ugliness around them and replace it with beauty, we then would reflect the effect of this beauty upon our minds.

What is it that inspires a thing of great beauty? Why are some people capable of this and others not? First you must have a very old and wise soul. An animal cannot create, a primitive soul cannot create with refinements, a young soul cannot create with subtlety. But very old souls who have been this route time and time again and who have worked hard and diligently every time around, who have felt the longing for greater and greater achievement that results in the soul's expansion awareness and expression, these, and these alone, are the great artists and composers. These are the same men to whom intuition has not become extinct but who sense the power and wisdom of the divine forces and make them their own, not only to enrich their own lives but those of others. Before a man can be divinely inspired he must create within himself a container suitable for this inspiration both as to quality and quantity. The old rule holds even here, that you cannot pour a quart into a pint container. We might as well face the fact that we receive only what we are qualified to receive and that our rewards are proportionate to our efforts.

Our opportunities to learn and to serve are there to be picked up. We have only to be faithful and perseverant, with a strong determination to succeed. We cannot fail in our endeavors if we work hard and keep our goal in mind. With every day that passes we should stop and ask ourselves if we have accomplished something worthwhile, not just indulged ourselves but made a step forward. Any journey we take begins with the first step.

Everything has a price

It is wise to keep in mind that indulgence has its price. This is a lesson we must learn sooner or later; it is not an easy one and you must hold it up to the subconscious continually. Keep the memory of the price to be paid vividly in your mind. Your main object in daily life is to learn as much as you can along the way and enjoy it to the fullest, and enjoyment can be spoiled by over-indulgence. Moderation keeps the senses alert. Abstinence is just as foolish, but balance is enjoyable and gives you freedom.

We must make a real effort to remember the fact that we humans are so easily drawn into our animal natures which wander aimlessly to find food anywhere, but that true human accomplishment always has a destination and without a goal, the whole of this life will have hardly been worthwhile.

To make our lives more worthwhile we need a broad foundation. A pole that is too thin falls over easily. A pyramid can't fall over. To read good books, meditate, take an interest in the arts, look for ways to lighten another's burdens, and bring light and happiness into other lives, are good ways to broaden our foundation and make positive strides with our own Karma.

Fear of death must be overcome

Fear is one of the strongest of the negative aspects to be overcome. The fear of losing life is stronger than any other and is nothing to be ashamed of. Compare your fear to that of a man who is told he is to take a journey and is never coming back. He will be unwilling to leave quickly. If he has time to prepare, he will be more willing to go. The art of living should, of course, be inclusive of the willingness to take that journey. It sometimes takes the whole of a lifetime to learn, and understandably so, if one's whole lifetime has been filled with fear and negativity and one has made no effort at self enlightenment.

The next time you hear anyone speak of death, notice the way in which he seems to pale a little, the way his voice automatically drops to an almost hushed tone. Observe the way in which he will avert his glances away from you so that you might not notice the look of fear that has crept into his eyes. He knows the fear is there; he can tell by the sick feeling in his stomach and the way his heart seems to be doing strange things in his chest.

What a vast amount of tears, agony and misery have been wasted over the inevitable event of death. And we, we alone have made it that way out of our own ignorance and resulting fears.

Death has become a terrifying god whom we are always trying to find ways to placate and appease.

One day my sister had taken one of my books to her office to read during her lunch hour, and a co-worker, who happened to notice it in passing, made the remark, "You read the strangest books." My sister said "Strange? I don't think so. I'm interested in where I'm going and what's going to happen to me when I die, aren't you?" The reply was "Heavens no! I don't want to even think about it!" And her mind, like the minds of so many others when asked this question, fled into a dark, safe closet and quickly slammed the door!

It has always seemed to me to be of utmost importance to make sure that one's mind does not contain a dark closet wherein one can quickly jam the things he doesn't want to look at. It is surprising how quickly it can become a habit to run to this closet and chuck in all sorts of little odds and ends that seem to be misfits, considering what you were taught, and what you might like to believe. I have always felt that good mental health comes from a firm determination never to be tempted by this quick and easy way out.

In reality, it is not a way out—as we all know. Just observe a person who makes a practice of doing this, a person who has all sorts of skeletons and bogey men of every shape and size that he keeps hidden. What actually happens is that this area of the closet becomes bigger and bigger and more frightening and forbidding with every passing day. Shutting things up is both childish and brutalizing. All one needs to do is walk over to that closet, jerk open the door, grab the things firmly, throttle them soundly and nine times out of ten they will collapse and go slithering lifelessly to the floor, and you will be left standing there wondering what on earth it was you had been so afraid of all this time!

It would be curious to know how much longer our "cultured civilization" is going to continue to be intimidated by this so-called "death." Certainly we can't count on help from those who are exploiting and profiting from our terror.

If I were to drive up one of the main thoroughfares in our town for a distance of five miles, I could point out several churches of different denominations, all of which teach one thing in common: immortality of the soul. Yet how many people actually believe it, except perhaps superficially during one hour on Sunday? How many people do you know who believe in the soul's immortality to the point of making it their own?

When the concepts we are writing of in this book are presented to the average person, it is not too unusual to have him look at you rather strangely and have him ask incredulously, "Do you really believe that?" Some will even back off ten paces. It is difficult to remember that these are the same people who attend these very same churches where immortality of the soul is taught. Churches which owe their very existence to the fact that Christ rose from the dead!

A conflict arises in the people who fear death; they fear it but at the same time they think death brings a promise of escape from something unpleasant in their lives. If people could come to realize that you get out of nothing, escape nothing by dying, what a change you would see overnight in our everyday world! The short-cuts a man thoughtlessly takes to get to the top, the ruthlessness he can exhibit in order to gain an advantage—all would come to a screeching halt. If he could simply realize that everything must in the end be balanced out, he would think a long time before he raised a hand against his fellow man.

One shudders at the very thought of what some of our world's leaders, all through history, face or are going to have to face. Look at the atrocities committed in our own century. Those responsible for all the different evils in the last war will be the victims of the tragedies of tomorrow. The segregationists of today will be back as the persecuted of tomorrow. And so it will go on and on, until every last soul is at last aware that there is more to the development of the soul than the life here and now.

The Eastern religions teach that "When we die we cannot take one minute particle of this physical world with us, nor can we leave behind one fragment of our mind." When we consider this, we can more easily understand the teaching that hell is of our own making and that the only way back is to retrace our steps, step by painful step.

Be careful of deceptions of life

One of the great dangers is that things in life can be so deceptive. What at first glance seems to be so obvious very seldom is. One day as I was driving past an apple orchard, it occurred to me that this orchard could very well represent a lesson in life. As one looked at this scene, rows of trees, windfall apples strewn over the ground, his obvious thought would be to merely pick up the apples off the ground. Yet, why be content with the apples on the ground that are very likely bruised and probably wormy, when with just a little effort one could stretch up and pluck a nice red, solid, juicy one. One would probably feel the better for the effort; the stretching feels good, and the accomplishment feels good. The strangest thing of all to contemplate is that the person who is content to settle for less because it seems the easiest is also the one who ends up with the backache, and the wormy, rotten apples as well. When you liken the apples to the fruits of life, it makes you pause to consider carefully what you want to settle for.

If we would stop long enough in our rushing around to realize what we could achieve with a little effort, a little stretching here and there, what great things could be gained: a sense of usefulness, endless progress and achievement, the ability to scale limitless heights. We could then build on every new experience, measure up to the fullest of our potential, and fully realize the radiant possibilities of the soul.

If you should find yourself looking at someone situated more fortunately than you and longing for the same advantages, don't get bogged down in the destructive emotion of envy. With the principles of reincarnation and Karma to build on, nothing is unattainable if you are willing to work. You may seemingly be trapped in a place or a particular situation, but if you use your time wisely and approach the problem with the proper attitude, you may well turn your straw into threads of gold, as in the nursery rhyme.

Let your frustration and longings work for you. Take your threads of gold and make yourself a garment beautiful beyond description. Don't be ashamed of these emotions of longing. The greatest pieces of music ever heard, the greatest works of poetry and literature ever written were created by people who mentally saw themselves standing on a high hill with their arms flung wide and saying "Oh dear God I wish!" "Oh, how I want to be able to . . . . !"

Free will and destiny

If the day is dull and you're wanting some stimulating conversation, try bringing up the subjects of free will and destiny. There is nothing that will change an apathetic group of people into soapbox orators any faster than these subjects are guaranteed to do. You will notice that even those who have never expressed an opinion on anything ever before, suddenly become all-knowing. This is probably because these particular subjects mean so many different things to so many different people. For some people they mean, I, me, ego decides every thing; for others they mean when we come upon crossroads in life, merely the right to choose a particular road that has struck our fancy.

Have you ever thought about all the things that go into the making of every single decision you make? Think about it for awhile and you will find a whole set of miracles staring you in the face.

Every thing that you now are is but the sum total of all your thoughts and experiences, slowly molded, shaped and re-molded through all the ages. Add the influences of heredity, and certainly environment, and then of course, friends, relations, enemies, and circumstances. Doesn't it strike you, then, as a colossal assumption to think that this particular ego in this particular moment of time, did all the deciding?

For as long as I can remember I have had a very simple picture that does a pretty good job of explaining the seeming paradox of free will and destiny, at least to my satisfaction. I have always seen these forces together, as a large wheel, with many spokes, the hub in the center representing the ultimate reality or God. When we are born, this when and where is decided by what has gone before in previous lives, by what still needs to be learned, what problems we have yet to work out, and several other factors. But when it is decided, we are then set down upon one of these spokes at the outer circumference, headed towards the center and given a gentle push. The die is cast, the pattern is set. As we travel down this particular spoke of the wheel, we can see that there are many on this same road with us, but we can also see across to all the other spokes of the wheel and observe all the other travelers busily plodding along their own particular paths. Now, although we can easily see all these other paths, there is no possible way we can cross over to them no matter how hard we try. That is for them and this is for you. This is your destiny! And keep in mind, it is of your own making.

Free will enters the picture in what you decide to do while you are on this road and how you decide to behave. When you come upon a very large boulder on your road, which is obstructing your path, you must make the decision whether to go around it, or put forth a little more effort and climb over it because it is the shorter way. This is free will in action.

Free will also means deciding upon how you are going to act when you meet a fellow traveler. Are you going to elbow him out of the way, bash him over the head, or turn, pause, and extend that helping hand? Should the last be how you decide to use your free will, it will do miraculous things for your destiny and your Karma. You must, however, keep in mind that lending a helping hand is one thing, and superimposing your will on that of another person and taking over the whole operation is quite another, for by so doing you are retarding his growth and causing his spiritual muscles to be weakened.

It is usually the sin of pride that causes us to take such a virtue as lending a helping hand and create a problem out of it. All because we think we know better, or our way of doing things is the best way. This is a common problem in human relationships and the way to avoid it is to "know thyself." Always ask yourself first, "Who am I really doing this for, for him or for my own glorification?"

Once again we come to the problem of balance in seeking self-enlightenment. This is not to be done to the point of neglect of duty, no matter how lofty your aims. There is nothing that surpasses doing the best you can in your own little corner of the world. A life of productive activity serves in itself as a prayer and, to my way of thinking, is far better than a life of so-called devotion that consists in spending hours in self scrutiny, idle contemplation and forced supplication. Christ said "Work *and* Pray," not either/or. An active life is usually a healthy one and gives others of your substance.

Say what you will, all the mental and spiritual activities of any person are unbelievable. If you make a decision about anything, what makes you make that one, and not another? Usually you are believing one set of miracles and rejecting another. What makes you grow and live? Is that not a miracle in itself? Just because it is an accepted fact doesn't make it any the less so. Look at our today's world. Astronauts are orbiting the earth. You can't give all the credit to just the mechanical device alone. It is the prayers and work and imagination of millions of men. Can we say that these are merely the mechanical results of physical laws? What is the origin of these laws? Do you understand them all, in detail?

There is so much today that is accepted as fact, which only a hundred years ago would have been rejected as fantasy and two hundred years ago would have been condemned as witch-craft.

Keep an open mind on everything that cannot be explained. Make certain of facts; be sure you *have* a fact and not an illusion. *But* if you have a fact that cannot be explained away, accept it courageously.

Chapter 8

Medical Hypnosis

There is no more blasphemous misuse of the human organism than the nightclub stage act utilizing hypnosis to get people to do idiotic things before an audience for idle amusement. I feel that the Creator did not include the wonderful subconscious portion of human minds in his act of creation for such stupid, meaningless usage. Rather than misusing the hyper-suggestibility of the subconscious in the entertainment field, why not put it to practical use in everyday living as every other species of animal does?

Hypnosis is not a panacea for all ailments; it is not an all-encompassing magic that can cure all ills; in fact "it" is not an "it" at all, not an entity unto itself. Hypnosis is a wonderful medical tool that has been too long ignored and too long allowed to dwell in the bungling hands of the psychoceramics (crack-pots). The ivory tower of academic medicine is just now teetering giddily on the border of accepting hypnosis as a medical tool.

As with all medical tools (scalpel, forceps, etc.), when in the hands of fools, irresponsible, immoral individuals, or criminals, they can result in harm. Don't blame this on the tool. The same instrument in the hands of a skilled, moral, dedicated operator can serve to heal, to alleviate pain, to lead one along the path of self-awareness, to righteous wholesomeness and purposeful, pro-ductive living.

Hypnosis is utilized in comprehensive medicine which considers human beings as consisting of three interrelated parts, (1) body, (2) mind, and (3) soul, and treats them accordingly.

What is hypnosis?

I'm not sure. I have used it as a doctor and observed other doctors using it for the past eighteen years, and I'm not sure just exactly what it is. This does not keep it from being used and useful. I'm not sure just exactly what electricity is either but I put it to a lot of uses.

Hypnosis is said to be an altered state of awareness associated with physical relaxation, mental concentration, narrowing or focusing of attention, and is characterized by hyper-suggestibility of behavior. *More simply it has been labeled consciousness of the subconscious.*

Like natural childbirth—the human mimicking of other animals in their conduct of labor—I can't adequately define it, I don't actually know *how* it works (nor, I believe, does anyone else) but I am a practicing doctor and I jolly well know *that* it works. The same holds for medical hypnosis. I have used this tool to help hold marriages together in marriage counseling; to resolve subconscious fears of pregnancy and achieve fertility in the formerly childless woman; to replace an inferiority complex with self confidence; to displace guilt and substitute for it responsibility; to change rejection of femininity to "I like being a girl"; to restore lost faith in the meaning of life; to change a fear of death (according to some psychiatrists, the basis cause of many psychoses) into the concept of death as the great adventure.

My first awareness of medical hypnosis came in the form of an invitation to dinner in 1947 when the first newspaper publicity came out regarding natural childbirth. My host was a fellow obstetrician who had been using hypnosis in obstetrics for years, and after reading about the unmedicated spontaneous births of our experimental nurse mothers, he welcomed me with open arms as a fellow medical hypnotist.

I was a most bewildered young intern. I didn't know what on earth he was talking about. I didn't know what medical hypnotists were but this chap seemed sure that whatever they are, I was one. The intern's salary then was fifteen dollars a month, and one who has subsisted long on a university hospital's "chow" doesn't turn down any offers to a decent dinner.

I feel now as I did then, that hypnosis can be used in obstetrics but that to use it is comparable to shooting a cannon at a sparrow when a "B-B" gun would suffice.

The "B-B" gun of natural childbirth is a form of prenatal education approached on the purely conscious level. It suffices beautifully and can be conveniently taught in large groups or learned from a book.[1] There may be an element of suggestion involved, but is this not so in all education—and church services? And if so, is this bad? Do not confuse hypnosis with mere suggestion. Almost all human behavior could be attributed to the use of suggestion.

Hypnosis for natural childbirth

The first stage of labor (sleep imitation) wherein the mother is taught to physically relax and mentally detach herself, appears to have much in common with hypnosis but only during the one-minute duration of uterine contractions. Between these contractions (and in the other stages of labor) the mother does not appear to be in any trance state; she is bright-eyed and alert. During the contractions the concentrated relaxation based on sleep imitation *appears* similar to the hypnotic trance to the casual observer. The argument is purely one of semantics, and I personally don't think it matters one bit whether the mother is hypnotized or not because who is the "operator" at this time? Her *husband!* One of the criticisms of hypnosis by a few religionists and inexperienced doctors is that the operator creates an emotional dependency in the subject.

In husband-coached natural childbirth such emotional dependency would be that of wife upon husband—as it should be! I wish all wives were more emotionally dependent upon their husbands, especially at this significant moment of their lives together, the birth of their children.

My host at dinner was so smugly sure I was a medical hypnotist, that I decided I'd better find out what on earth I was.

The more I investigated, the more curious I became. Now, many years later, medical hypnosis has made great strides and is here to stay. It is not necessary for obstetrics but has proven very useful in many, many other ways when properly utilized.

---

[1] Robert A. Bradley, *Husband-Coached Childbirth* (New York: Harper & Row Publishers, Inc., 1965).

Cause of mental conflicts

Conflicts between the subconscious and the conscious levels of awareness constitute a frequently unrecognized cause of many human problems. When these conflicts are recognized, explored, understood and then resolved we have the true solution to the problem and often dramatic results. Any therapeutic approach short of this represents plugging one's ears with cotton in order not to hear the knock in the engine, whereas hypnotic exploration of the subconscious compares with systematic disassembling of the engine until the "conflict" is found, then correcting it.

Cause of infertility

The field of infertility treatment would serve to illustrate the importance of such an approach.

We will enlarge on mind affecting the body in greater detail in a subsequent chapter of psychosomatics. However, a short illustration is necessary here. In my experience with infertility cases of couples who have been married for years, are not using contraceptives and consciously desire children, but have none, over eighty percent of my cases show no recognizable physical cause for the failure of conception.

No one really knows how emotions and the subconscious produce the actual effect of limiting or blocking fertility. Again, as happens so often, we are not intellectually advanced enough to know *how,* only that it *occurs.*

A doctor acquaintance who had spent many years in China some time ago, described his observation that many young and therefore presumably fertile women of low social status would serve for years as prostitutes with no protection from pregnancy. They would diligently save their earnings until they had accumulated enough to serve as a dowry when they would elevate their social status by "purchasing" an acceptable husband. During the years of exposure no pregnancies ensued. Shortly after marriage and social acceptance as a wife, pregnancies occurred regularly.

In my pre-hypnosis days I recall one Christmas season when, probably affected by the holiday spirit, I felt sorry for three couples who had faithfully gone through a "complete" infertility study but to no avail. I gave up, told *them* to give up, and arranged adoption of others' babies. All three women became pregnant the very next cycle. Why? How? Was my infertility treatment really "complete?" I felt very foolish and very medically inept. Today, no infertility study is complete, in my estimation, without hypnotic exploration of the subconscious. Becoming aware of this, I began to study these women's emotional as well as physical make-up.

In some cases no great emotionally fraught situation was uncovered. Some cases were simply a matter of the woman trying too hard. They were so preoccupied with wanting a baby so badly that they were all internally "tied up in knots." This can result in spasm of not only their intestinal tracts (producing spastic colons, ulcers, etc.) but also apparently their Fallopian tubes, resulting in relative sterility. This has been directly demonstrated, utilizing hypnosis, by observation of these tubes with a special instrument. Under the effect of conscious social stresses they appeared as pale, rigid, motionless tubes. With the application of hypnosis to release conscious stresses and achieve subconscious awareness the tubes can be seen changing. They become pink, relaxed, and gently waving instead of rigid. A sudden verbal command to return to the conscious "awake" state and the tubes snap back to their former pale, rigid, motionless appearance.

In the cases where hypnosis showed the problem to be simply trying too hard, becoming obsessed with the idea of having a baby, the hypersuggestibility of the subconscious was utilized to give a post hypnotic suggestion of "I don't care if I have a baby or not."

I wanted them to itemize all the other wonderful privileges living bestowed and suggested that they would cheerfully accept babies if they came but equally accept the situation if they did not. What will be, will be. Quit trying to control destiny. If the patient was well oriented spiritually, the suggestion was strengthened by the approach of "God's will be done" or "Quit telling God how to do His work!" Conception still is in the category of an act of God, not the will of man, even in a court of law. Count your blessings (other than babies) and be grateful for what you have instead of longing for what you have not, and so forth.

Case history of wilful infertility

In other instances, upon exploring the subconscious we would run into a veritable hornet's nest, rather than a simple over-desire. For instance: I recall one very hostile lady who defiantly marched into our office for treatment of infertility. She immediately launched into a tirade of condemnation of specialists who treat infertility. "You're the fourth doctor I've been to in as many states. I've had all your miserable tests and I'm still not pregnant. I've spent hundreds of dollars and have nothing to show for it. What's the matter with you guys? Don't you know your business?"

Such transference of responsibility, such over-aggressive hositility on a conscious level bespoke of turmoil on a subconscious level. It took only a light hypnotic trance and a gentle question, "Do you *really* want to get pregnant?" to release a tirade of bitterness bottled up in the subconscious. "I'll never get pregnant as long as that old (w)itch of a mother-in-law keeps hounding me! 'When are you going to bear my son a child?' (Sneeringly repeated.) I'll never get pregnant, I'll show that old bat!"

After a few long sessions of hypnosis, age-regressing to find the origin of this over-resentment of authority, post hypnotic suggestions were given to "grow up," pointing out the childishness, the immaturity of her resentment. It was further suggested that *she* was important, her *husband* and her life with him was important, her mother-in-law was not in the least important. Her husband was instructed to purchase a set of mother-in-law earrings for her to wear as a reminder whenever his mother visited. The word "IN" was printed on one earring and the word "OUT" on the other! Results: Deeper relationship between man and wife, a self maturation process by the wife, and not long afterwards the blessing of a baby.

Fear as hypnotic reality

Probably the largest number of subconscious blocks interfering with fertility would fall in the category of subconscious fear of pregnancy.

With all the old wives' tales of horrible deliveries combined with the bridge table gossip wherein each woman tends to embroider her own "suffering" to impress her friends, a woman yet to experience childbirth would have to be a complete moron not to have some degree of anxiety associated with the act of childbearing. Careful education on a conscious level in prenatal classes or from an educated husband can counteract these old wives' tales by an appeal to logic.

However, there are so many fears so deeply buried in the subconscious from early childhood, so many negative experiences that conscious-leveled education cannot reach, that hypnotic subconscious approach is necessary in some cases.

An example of this occurred in our practice. An attractive teenage wife came in for the first time, fearful of being pregnant. Her countenance from the very first showed fear and anxiety. Her restless hands kept clutching and unclutching a handkerchief dripping with nervous perspiration. She sat on the very edge of the chair during the history taking, every muscle defensively tightened.

Like most obstetricians I take great pride in the medical art of proper management, putting such young ladies at ease and seeing their rigidity change to relaxation, seeing the stiff embarrassment change to jocularity in the course of the office visit. However, in this particular case all my medical art went for naught. I simply could not get results. After a careful exam, performed in spite of her board-like rigidity, it was obvious that she was pregnant. I verbally congratulated her that I had found nothing medically "wrong" but rather something beautifully "right"—she was going to have a baby! Instead of the usual expression of delight normally expected, this young lady became even more rigid, her eyes became glassy with mental disorientation, and I had to actually carry her, like a log, to the hospital for admission and consultation by a psychiatrist. Her diagnosis—hysteria based upon fear of pregnancy. After deep sedation it took diligent age regression under hypnosis to find the "knocks" in this engine that represented such a dreadful fear of what should be life's most rewarding experience. We had to go back until the age of four before the causative "blip" was encountered.

She had lived in another city as a child and her house when she was four years old was directly across the street from the maternity section of a "Mercy Hospital." In the warm climate there the windows of the maternity wing were left open. She had been frightened out of her wits by the horrible screams of the medicated maniacs, mothers who were unprepared for childbirth and had had what little self control they possessed from instinct knocked away by medication and the wildness it produced. These were the old days of scopolamine jags. This drug supposedly produced amnesia, so the suffering mothers would forget the "dreadful experience" of becoming mothers. In doses heavy enough to produce amnesia, the side effects of mental disorientation and excitation produced this horror that carried itself to the innocent ears of an impressionable child across the street. I think that the hospital was most appropriately named, "Mercy"!

The terror stricken little girl had run for reassurance to her mother crying, "Mama, Mama, they're killing somebody over there!" Her mother, in abysmal ignorance of the thin layer of conscious over-lay at this tender age which exposes the hypersuggestible subconscious mind, answered, "Oh, that's just women having babies. I sure hope that never happens to my little girl."

The searing deep scar made by this "motherly" suggestion on this open little mind was not easily erased. It took every device in our medical bag to convincingly counteract such preconditioning for motherhood. The further back in age the scars are made, the harder they are to erase. Also, the more the one making the suggestion is accepted, at that time, as an authoritarian figure—as someone who really knows all the answers—the harder the scar is to erase. In this case we were dealing with the most authoritarian of all figures to a four-year-old—mother.

Hypnotic suggestion, as we said, is not all-encompassing. The addition of suggestions to the surface of the subconscious by a mere doctor helped but could not entirely counteract the deep fright-evoked mother-suggestion of early life. I didn't think we were getting anywhere. She simply did not believe that childbirth could possibly be a pleasant, rewarding, unmedicated experience shared, pleasurably, with her husband. She didn't believe it, that is, until her wondering eyes were allowed to observe repeated husband-coached natural childbirths. This was more convincing than all the verbal suggestions on earth, to be there and to actually share in other couples' joy at the birth of their children. The excitement, the pride in accomplishment, the intimacy of shared love between a man and his wife with this new, wonderful type of childbirth is so contagious that it brings uncontrolled tears of shared happiness to the eyes of even the most hardened of individuals.

This young lady and her attentive, loving husband became another birth team that produced a new baby girl, joyfully and proudly by husband-coached, shared childbirth. A baby girl that will grow up to become not only a good citizen but an emotionally well adjusted mother herself some day, whose obstetrician will have no "extras" to perform in preparing her for motherhood.

Hypnosis in marriage counseling

Marriage counseling is another aspect of treatment to which hypnosis therapy spontaneously led. I had no intention of becoming involved in this field and had regularly directed troubled couples to the established counselors for care. They kept bouncing back. The high incidence of *unmarried* marriage counselors insulted the intelligence of our patients. It amounted, even with the few married ones, to another debator joining in on the argument *on a conscious level* and everyone aimlessly batting around his views of the superficial results of subconscious conflicts, but no one, no one, getting down to the basic cause!

Having established a rapport with these couples through childbearing, and feeling strongly about the pitiful inadequacy of marriage counseling in general (consider the national divorce rate!) I applied the principle of exploring the subconscious via hypnosis to find the true underlying cause of marital conflicts, and again found clinical justification for the hypothesis.

This book is not intended to teach techniques of hypnosis—there are volumes in any library which adequately cover this. However, I must add one explanation of technique here which was adopted from the work and writings of David B. Cheek, M.D. This involves what is referred to as ideomotor activity of the mind in relation to the body.

To illustrate: Most people consciously know whether they are right-handed or left-handed. However, most people do not consciously know if they are right-footed or left-footed. They would have to think that over and then may not be sure. A simple way of discovering this, especially if the one being tested is standing on a fine, finished flooring in his own home, would be to suddenly and unexpectedly drop a lighted match on the floor at his feet. Whichever foot he used to meet the emergency and stamp out the fire would give the answer. He did not say to himself consciously, "Now let me see, which foot will I use," but without the delay of conscious involvement, his subconscious directed a physical action.

Such physical action representing the subconscious can be capitalized upon to demonstrate conflicts between the subconscious and conscious mind. With the patient in a light trance, instruction is given to raise the index finger of the right hand to signify the answer "Yes" and the index finger of the left hand for "No." A series of simple questions are given until the patient becomes accustomed to this routine. Then both verbal and finger answers are requested. As the past is explored, careful observation is made for any variance between verbal and finger answers. The verbal has often been found to be representative of conscious processing or even superficial subconscious processing of the answers, whereas the unconscious movement of the finger may reflect the true deeper subconscious level. Also, the depth of trance will vary continuously as will similarly overlapping conscious coloring. This variation is affected by the emotional content of the questions or by a fundamental trait of hypnosis which is little understood—that trance depth is continuously fluctuating, never static.

In marriage counseling conscious cover-up can become evident when the mouth says "Yes" and the finger says "No." The movement of the finger may be only slight, just a flicker, but is significant. The patient can be instructed to discontinue the use of the fingers and to respond verbally, yet, will still show finger activity unconsciously, especially if conflict or strong emotions are associated with the question. This is more helpful to the operator than it is essential. It simply is a short-cut to the areas of conflict and cuts down the time involved.

Utilizing this simple technique, unsuspected subconscious irritations, resentment of criticism, feelings of being dominated, suppressed, etc., have been uncovered, recognized, discussed and resolved to help young people adjust to each other.

The medical management of problems of frigidity, menopause, tension headaches, compulsive eating, stuttering, allergic disorders, etc., can all be handled similarly. Age regression is done to find out past methods of handling stress, relationship to parents, siblings, peers, etc., then purposeful suggestions can be made which are appropriate to the problem.

Can everyone be hypnotized?

A question frequently asked is, can everyone be hypnotized? In the first place I don't like the implication that someone is doing something to someone else. I feel all hypnosis to be a form of self-hypnosis. The hypnotist plays a role similar to that of a football coach who doesn't actually play football. His help is efficient and convenient to be sure that someone else is performing properly. The actual altered awareness of the hypnotic trance is self-produced. I strongly feel that every human like all other animals can similarly alter his awareness—if adequately motivated.

The nightclub hypnotist has everyone in the audience hold up one hand—then he soothingly speaks slower, and slower, and lower in tone, then suddenly commands, "Now, you cannot lower your arm, try and see!" About seventeen percent of the hands will remain up, the others are lowered. He then selects his subjects from the seventeen percent to put on his act. Obviously, about seventeen percent of humans are hypnoidal, or suggestible. It is interesting that about this same number of humans present spontaneous evidence of some type of "Psi" ability in E.S.P. They can not only make themselves aware of their own subconscious but can and do utilize its functions.

Now, what about the other eighty-three percent? Well, they can be hypnotized and will manifest E.S.P., but there has to be greater motivation. Motivation is important. Animals who live in a predatory environment are very well motivated. The possum plays possum to keep from being killed. The pheasant or quail "freezes" to keep from being seen and killed. Other animals use E.S.P. to sense danger or to select a safe action—if they don't learn to accurately utilize all their perceptive abilities, they will be killed. Natural selection is on the side of E.S.P. ability.

I hope the test will never be necessary, but it has been surmised that should an atomic holocaust or other catastrophe occur that would revert humans back to a predatory, uncivilized existence, the "extra" sensory functions of their subconscious minds which lie idly dormant and unneeded in a civilized world would "break through" to the front to be utilized again—*if necessary to prevent being killed.* Could it be that the oracles of biblical times were more accurate than modern ones are today because of motivation? In ancient times, men lived a lush high position of power if their predictions were right, and got their heads removed abruptly if they were wrong. Rather stimulating motivation! I have a feeling that if we were under such conditions, more than seventeen percent of us would demonstrate precognition. I'll also conjecture that if you or I were trapped in some situation where there was a surgeon available but no anesthesia to be had other than hypnosis and we developed an acute appendicitis to the point that our life depended on surgery, we would become hypnoidal very, very rapidly. Any of us.

Here again I criticize the usual academic parapsychology experiments in E.S.P. The multitudinous "controls" destroy that which they purport to test—they bore the subjects to death; they have little or no motivation to score. I would like to see the armed forces highly motivate volunteers in experiments by granting them extended leave, special attractive duty, etc., if they produced high Psi scores, and no favors if they didn't.

Again, hypnosis is a medical instrument. Be very careful to consider the skill, training, and background of the operator who uses it.

When properly used, the subconscious mind with its wonderful powers can be put to daily use for man's benefit for which it was designed. By more fully "knowing thyself," one can learn to "like thyself" and the inner light resulting will so shine that it will be evident to all.

As a practicing physician the matter of hypnosis, then, is a practical tool to be put to daily use. It can also be a research instrument serving to explore the depth of the total personal agent. A glimpse of such usage was obtained in our illustration of age regression beyond birth, reliving past lives. There is a great need for controlled experimentation bringing up foreign language knowledge, not acquired in this life; obtaining evidential material via recent reincarnations with correlation of birth and death certificates; measuring perceptual abilities enhanced by expansion under subconscious levels.

Inducing negative hypnosis

A new frontier is available here in the use of negative hallucination hypnotically induced. We have heard of an experiment of this nature demonstrating clairvoyance. It is not first-hand material as we are not familiar with the source, but why is it not academically reported?

Post hypnotic suggestion can be utilized—as it is by the nightclub hypnotist—to make people *not* hear, see, smell, touch or taste some specified target upon awakening. This is called producing negative hallucination. By suggestion you can fool the conscious mind into not seeing a particular person, or into a conviction that that person is not here, or doesn't exist. In the nightclub act the subject will try to sit in a chair already occupied by this person and the genuine conscious bewilderment evident when the subject realizes some unseen body is already occupying the chair they are trying to sit down in, sends the audience into peals of laughter.

I think such hallucination is fascinating, rather than funny, and should be utilized to teach and learn more about the mind. For instance, the experiment we have heard about involved giving a negative hallucination suggestion to the subject, that he would not see Mr. Jones, there was no Mr. Jones.

Then Mr. Jones was caused to enter the room carrying a long stemmed rose behind his back which was out of conscious visual range of the subject. Mr. Jones' body hid the flower from the subject's view. The subject did not see Mr. Jones but saw through him and cried out in genuine conscious amazement to see a rose floating through the room unsupported!

Let's transfer this phenomena of hypnotically induced hallucination from the stage to the laboratory. Seek out people capable of the deepest trances and conduct purposeful, planned programs of experimentation. There is so much that could be done. When I suggested utilizing hypnosis for such purposes to medical leaders at hypnosis conventions, they shuddered and backed off, exclaiming, "We have trouble enough getting peer and public acceptance of hypnosis itself. Don't rock the boat with E.S.P." Some of these same leaders admit privately to similar experiences with hypnosis accidently manifesting extra-sensory phenomena, but, having just gotten the "powers that be," as we have said before, teetering giddily on the verge of making hypnosis legitimate, they do not want it associated with any other yet-to-be-accepted field. Professional politics also protrudes its ugly nose to make peevish children out of what should be honest scientific men. Instead of presenting a united front, little factions appear clustering childishly about different so-called leaders, each faction jealously trying to outdo the other for recognition.

All is not lost. Great truths will survive such pettiness. Medical hypnosis although still in its infancy, is a rapidly growing child and is here to stay.

Chapter 9

Dependence of Body on Mind

We have stressed how the mind (subconscious) is capable of leaving the body during life and how it continues of itself after bodily death. Superficially, this might suggest that the mind has not much to do with the physical body, yet nothing could be further from fact; the mind has a great deal to do with the body. *It behooves you to be very aware of how your mind can affect your body and see to it that this effect is beneficial rather than harmful.*

The subconscious "animal" portion of the human brain houses the seat of the emotions. Emotional upsets can be deleterious (or negative) to bodily functions.

The Thanksgiving turkey is roasting and sending out its delicious fragrances, the family is gathered together looking forward hungrily to the impending sumptuous holiday dinner when suddenly, the doorbell rings. A telegram is presented telling of the unexpected, sudden death of a loved one. The emotional impact of the saddening news upon their physical bodies will affect each one's gastric motility, gastric secretions, rate of heart beat, state of metabolism (changing physical exuberance to lethargy), etc. The ravenous appetite that preceded the telegram changes to "I'm not very hungry."

In a more gradual but just as effective way, the promotion that was undeservedly (you thought) given to the other worker instead of you; the feeling of being trapped in a rut without being able to get ahead; the mother-in-law who moves in, or next door,

and constantly criticizes; the thought of the education you could
have had, had you not married so young, or had the baby not
come so soon; any of these subconscious thoughts can also
interfere with gastric motility resulting in delayed emptying of the
stomach and the production of ulcers (digesting yourself) from
retained stomach acid.

The young lady who all her life heard her disgruntled mother
complain of the woman's sorry lot in life—men have it easy!—will
gradually resent her husband and reject her own femininity along
with all the manifestations of it. Her menses will be referred to as
the "curse" that women must bear and will result in incapacitat-
ing, violent cramps of the rejected organ each month. This is not
imagination; the uterine cramps are like the hole in the stomach
(ulcer), very physically real, but the *cause* is mental, the *result* is
physical.

Hypnosis and psychosomatic cases

When I first utilized hypnosis in dealing with my patients'
problems, I dutifully used it only on the obviously mentally or
emotionally based cases. However, as time has passed, it became
increasingly evident that nothing is purely physical. There is an
emotional or mental overlay to *everything* physical. An aspect of
this was demonstrated very effectively at a medical hypnosis
convention by the report of an armed forces orthopedic physician
who presented a study of the effect of hypnotic suggestion on the
rate of healing of fractures of the femur, the large bone of the hip.

For purposes of study he had given "positive" suggestions and
"negative" suggestions to alternate fracture cases in hypnotic
trances, then studied the results. The positive suggestions were that
as soon as this fracture heals the individual would be transferred to
the most ideal assignment (For example, south-sea islands plus
beautiful girls!) and the negative suggestions were that the next
duty would be most non-ideal (Adak, Aleutians, plus no girls!).
You can guess which group of fractures healed the most rapidly!
There was not only a statistically calculable difference, but it was
so dramatic that X-rays were presented actually showing the
remarkably rapid rate of healing of the bone—in the "positive"
group.

At this same convention a burn and blister was effected on a
young lady's forearm by touching it with a cool pencil eraser while

she was in trance and with the suggestion that it was hot and would burn. What does it take to convince people that the human mind affects the human body? Medical hypnotists first tried to convince the public by producing anesthesia in small local areas of the body and performing minor surgery. They were met with skepticism. Gradually larger areas were affected, still they were met with public doubt. Finally, in desperation the doctors cried out, "What do you want for proof, major surgery?" The answer was "Yes," always with the skeptical public anticipating failure. So medical hypnotists obligingly performed major surgery utilizing hypnosis as the only anesthetic. They did Cesarean sections, hysterectomies, thyroidectomies, etc., yet still the public doubted.

A medical colleague compared this problem of enlightening the public with that of a psychiatrist who was trying to convince a schizophrenic patient that he was not dead. The patient was firmly convinced that he *was* dead. The psychiatrist in desperation asked, "Do dead people bleed?" The patient answered, "Why, no." The doctor then cleansed the patient's index finger with alcohol, jabbed in a needle, and held the bleeding puncture wound up before the owner. He looked, then remarked brightly, "Gee, why dead people *do* bleed, don't they?"

The deliberate use of suggestion for anesthesia in major surgery was preceded by some instances of accidental, unintentional use. One surgeon reported an operation in which he was suturing the incision closed and remarked to his anesthetist to compliment him on his effective use of drugs to keep the patient asleep and muscles relaxed. He stated, "That was a good anesthetic, doctor," as he busily placed the final stitches. Both the surgeon and anesthetist were startled to hear the patient briskly agree, "It certainly was!" She wasn't asleep at all. Her inability to feel pain was a state of body resulting from a state of mind, not from being put to sleep by medication.

Another case was reported wherein the anesthetist was preparing a mother for a Cesarean section necessitated by hemorrhage from a low lying placenta. The anesthetist had strapped the gas mask on the patient's face but was administering only pure oxygen (to help the baby) while he busily changed a depleted gas tank on his machine before beginning the anesthetic. As he finished adjusting the new full tank of anesthetic gas and turned to start the anesthetic, he was amazed in looking over the shielding drape to see the surgeon holding up the baby he had just removed from the incision. There had not been a peep from the mother—she had been "put to sleep" with pure oxygen. Both the surgeon and the mother had assumed that the mask on her face represented anesthetic gas actually being given. The psychosomatic (mind affecting body) result was just as effective. In fact it was more effective as there were no side effects from medication: lowered blood pressure, intestinal upsets, inability to empty the bladder, long recovery "hangover," etc. The embarrassed anesthetist never said a word or administered any other gas. The remainder of the operation was performed without event and the patient "awakened" when the oxygen mask was removed.

The subconscious not dependent on conscious

The subconscious mind can affect the body without the conscious mind realizing it in other ways, as demonstrated by the studies of Dr. Eckhard H. Hess. Dr. Hess, a psychologist, first described the phenomena of the pupil of the eye dilating in association with interest or pleasure and constricting with frustration or displeasure.[1] The fact that this action is beyond conscious control and beyond conscious awareness constitutes a wonderful new tool for the study of the subconscious minds of humans and even lower animals. In a later article[2] Dr. Hess and associates aptly demonstrated the practical use of this subconscious physical effect by accurately classifying hetero- or homosexual men according to their pupil response to looking at pictures of nude men or women. How much human misery could be prevented if this test was required of all applicants for marriage licenses. It could also be used as an accurate lie detector in suspected criminals, the pupil dilating at appropriate pictures if guilty of the crime and unaffected if innocent. Here is a short-cut to the subconscious, not only more rapid than psychoanalysis from conscious association, but also more accurate. It should be used to screen all prospective teachers, especially of elementary levels, to see if they truly (subconsciously) like children.

---

[1] E. H. Hess and J. M. Polt, "Pupil Size as Related to Interest Value of Visual Stimuli," *Science,* 1960, pp. 132, 349-350.

[2] E. H. Hess, A. L. Seltzer, and J. M. Shlien, "Pupil Response of Hetero- and Homosexual Males to Pictures of Men and Women," *Journal of Abnormal Psychology,* 1965, Vol. 70, No. 3, pp. 165-168.

How the body reflects the mind

The body physically reflects the content of the mind in many other more subtle ways. The selfish, grasping miser suffers from chronic constipation. The doubting, distrusting old maid has thin tight blue lips and a pucker-string pattern of tension lines surrounding her selfish mouth. In contrast, the generous, motherly type of woman who continues to joyfully return her husband's love, whose main joy in life is giving rather than receiving—her mouth shows warmth and relaxed fullness in pink full lips, unrestrained by nervous tension lines.

The will to live, or to die, can directly affect the body. An elderly lady falls and breaks her hip. She is going to die. She doesn't die from a broken hip. The death certificate will list the cause as "pneumonia secondary to bed rest." But is that the true cause, or just the method of dying? In many cases the true cause is the wish to die. Her friends were all gone, she had outlived her relatives, and she simply had no reason to live.

Terminal pneumonia in the elderly, which in spite of all known treatment is setting its obvious, fatal path of steadily rising temperature and pulse rate, has been reported to dramatically reverse its course with hypnotic suggestions establishing earthly goals yet to be achieved, outlining reasons for continuing to live.

Such a will to live or die is not limited to the elderly. There are many reports from studies of aboriginal witch-doctors who put the evil eye of death upon young people who obligingly go home, lie down and die; of young people, like the young convict in the movie, *The Bird-Man of Alcatraz,* who although their injuries are minor and not serious proceed to die, from the lack of the will to live. Moreover, the subconscious mind, remember, is emotional, not logical; it can make mistakes. Sometimes these mistakes are beneficial, as in the case of the Cesarean section "anesthetic," but sometimes they can be harmful.

Such a harmful mistake, "by George," was related at a medical convention. It involved a doctor who was a specialist in urology (kidney problems). This doctor had been operated on due to an undiagnosed tumor or growth in his stomach. The patient, being a doctor himself, was preoccupied by the knowledge of the high likelihood of cancer in such growths. Fortunately the tumor had been found to be benign or non-cancerous upon an immediate microscopic examination (frozen section) performed by the pathology laboratory while the patient was still asleep. This rapid diagnosis was requested by the surgeon at the time of surgery as the tumor had grossly appeared to be suspicious of malignancy or cancer. It was not cancer, so a simpler operation was all that was required and the surgery was completed without event. However, the patient's kidneys refused to function after the operation. All kidney tests performed showed no evidence of abnormality; there was no medical explanation for the shut down. In desperation, after it became obvious that before long the patient would die from a kidney shut-down, a medical hypnotist was consulted.

Under age-regression, reliving the operation, playing back the subconscious memory tape, the patient relived hearing the operating room conversation—up to a point. The point where recall ceased was where the surgeon stated, upon removing the growth, "It looks suspicious. We'd better get a frozen section." The patient, being medically trained, subconsciously interpreted this statement as a diagnosis of cancer—which had been a prime conscious worry before surgery. But "George" is illogical, remember. His subconscious panicked, acted to block out further auditory awareness, and decided if he was going to die it would not be a long, lingering cancer death. He decided he might as well exercise a choice and "George" chose the one he was most familiar with, as a urologist, kidney shut-down. This actually is a comfortable way to go, by comparison, if one has to go.

The medical hypnotist recognized the problem, gave proper suggestions in the trance—"But you didn't wait to hear the pathological report. It was benign!" The patient's kidneys immediately resumed functioning and he recovered.

Again, we are not sufficiently advanced to know *how* the mind can affect the body; we only know *that* it does.

Hypnosis not accepted by religious organizations

Why must we wait until all else fails, to use hypnosis? Why must practicing doctors today still have to battle religionists whose faith is so flimsy they are afraid they'll lose it if they subject their minds to medical hypnosis? All is not lost. The more confident major religions have already sanctioned medical hypnosis as a God-given function of man's mind intended to be used for man's benefit.

Organized religions contribute a great deal by owning and

operating public hospitals. It is only when they restrict life-saving procedures from being used due to narrow religious beliefs that I feel they are unjustified being involved in the management of tax-exempt public institutions. Federal grants from taxation of the general public are used to help construct and support these hospitals with the understanding that they are to treat the entire public. On such a basis they are exempt from taxes; how can they then dictate to staff doctors that they cannot use medical hypnosis in the treatment of patients occupying these hospital beds?

Self-awareness of mind first step to health

Self-awareness of the interaction of the mind upon the body is the first step towards total health. Unaware patients will flounder from doctor to doctor unable to accept the gentle suggestion that their symptoms are manifestations of psychosomatic processes. They are insulted and walk away in a huff thinking the doctor implies "it's all in my head" or "it's just due to nerves." The idea that anything due to nerves could be a "just" appalls me.

That "just" should be more appropriately applied to physical ills. "Oh, it's *just* due to a tumor." We could, as doctors, easily remove the cause by surgery. Or, "Your pain is *just* due to infection," and we could give a prescription for antibiotics. This is the easy treatment. If the illness is due to "nerves," there is no simply "just" treatment. The doctor will have to take a few weeks a year out of his vacation time to take training in medical hypnosis in order to treat this condition adequately. He won't be able to "just" scribble off a prescription for pills; he will have to take a cut in his golf time and give the patient a few hours of careful study via hypnosis. While physical ills are boringly simple to manage, emotional ills are challengingly complex. Fellow doctors: accept the challenge of comprehensive medicine; don't just be mere pill rollers!

The misguided doctor-shopping patients seeking physical causes for their complaints become, subconsciously, very cunning and utilize what little medical knowledge they've gained to fool the next doctor by quoting symptoms related to specific organs. As a result, all non-essential organs are gradually nibbled away by multiple, unnecessary operations, and the patient remains unchanged, still floundering around looking vainly for a physical cause for mental effects.

All harmful physical effects are not necessarily indirect manifestations of subconscious conflicts. Some may be direct effects,
regardless of the presence or absence of conflicts. Direct effect is
illustrated by the burn and blister on the young lady's arm by
means of the pencil eraser. There may also be combinations of
indirect and direct effect. I think allergic reactions illustrate this
well. Subconscious conflicts may manifest themselves as skin
rashes—in people who inherit delicate skin—and as headaches (or
some other organ effect) in people whose physical inheritance is
thick, tough skin. Similarly, inherited delicacy of "inside skin,"
the living membranes of the eye, nose, sinuses, bronchial passages,
etc., may manifest subconscious conflicts *indirectly* as hayfever
and asthma. However, the simple fact may be also that this
inherited skin (external or internal) is actually so thin in nature
that a simple, direct irritating action can be produced by the pollen
irritant without any subconscious conflicts involved.

Subconscious conflicts in children

We have an outstanding hospital in Denver for treating
asthma in children. Cases have been reported in which the bronchial spasm of asthma represents the *indirect* manifestation of
subconscious conflicts. In one such case the asthmatic child,
when taken out of the home environment producing the conflict
(e.g., sibling jealousy, hostility towards parents, etc.) ceased to
have asthma the moment he walked through the door to live in the
hospital. The asthma would return immediately if he returned
home or, in another reported case, simply if he were told that his
mother was coming to visit.

But all asthma cases are not due to subconscious conflicts and
many will be unaffected by treatment that tried to find and resolve
such conflicts. Some may be *direct* effects due to inherited
physical characteristics. Can hypnosis help these too? Yes indeed,
but the therapeutic suggestions must be different in these instances.

Direct suggestion caused the pencil eraser to burn the lady's
forearm. Can mind-body effects of similar direct action be beneficial as well as harmful? Yes.

When, upon exploration, significant conflicts have failed to
appear, allergies can be treated by direct suggestion. This suggestion can be given by others or by self. I was able to break a

bronchial spasm in one of our children who suffered from severe asthma by the direct suggestion, as he was going to sleep, that his lungs were getting dryer and dryer, his breathing was getting easier and easier. It worked. Later on, he could give himself the same instructions and achieve the same result without the help of others. He even applied this same self-suggestion later to stop his nose from bleeding, much to the amazement of his soccer coach. When he got bumped and his nose bled he would decline the offer of a cotton nasal pack; curl up on the ground, close his eyes, concentrate and very efficiently stop the bleeding by self-suggestion.

Hypnosis for allergies

His mother also suffered from asthma and hay fever and was tested as 4+ allergic to 49 out of 50 mixed antigens injected into her skin. For years she followed all medical treatment prescribed by distinguished allergists—all to no avail. In desperation she decided one day, after becoming aware of hypnosis, that if others couldn't help her (she'd been through the whole gamut of treatment) she was obviously going to have to help herself—so she did. She curled up on her side, relaxed her body, then concentrated on a direct effect of dryness and relaxation of these affected areas with dramatic immediate relief. She further gave a determined self-suggestion that a return of the problem "simply isn't allowed." Many years have gone by; the allergy has not returned—"it wouldn't dare!" Whenever any member of the family sneezes or sniffs they get a humorous but effective maternal glare and the command "Stop it! We simply don't allow it!"

Physical symptoms, then, can be multiple and many and they can appear in nearly any organ of the body and in many variable forms: skin rashes, nasal irritations, eye irritations, bronchial spasms, headaches, high blood pressure, ulcers, muscle spasms, heart palpitations, constipation and/or diarrhea, menstrual cramps, backaches, etc., and the most commonly recognized physical manifestation of a mental attitude directed towards someone you disapprove of, a "pain in the neck."

All these physical manifestations can be compared to the visible portion of an iceberg: they may be only surface representations of deeper, greater, underlying portions. Trimming off the surface part that shows is ineffectual treatment since something will bob up elsewhere. The eczema of the skin that served as an excuse for the painfully shy, insecure teenage girl not to date boys will, if cleared up by medication, manifest itself elsewhere as migraine headaches or stomach cramps, etc. Don't just treat the symptoms, recognize and remove their cause.

Follow through on professional hypnosis care

Now, after succeeding in getting my patients to be aware of the possibility that their physical symptoms are surface manifestations of underlying mental processes, (and sometimes this is quite a task) lo and behold I have yet another problem. They think because it is mental that they should be able to handle it and solve it entirely themselves. The idea that I think they can't is taken as personal effrontery. They act as if there must be something deficient in someone who has to ask for outside help to clear up his or her psychosomatic problems.

Some will say "but I can do that for myself." Such intentions are good, but I have not been impressed by results. The very personality types who make this statement are usually the ones most in need of objective "outside" help. This is no reflection on the individual's intelligence or acumen; both may be of the highest order. Rather, it is a recognition that you cannot see yourself as others see you; that subconscious elements are truly subconscious; that you cannot see the woods for the trees about you. I like to make the comparison here that the individual is standing in the middle of the woods with multiple paths before him to choose from. Since he has not been down these paths before and since his view is restricted, he is not really sure where they lead. All he is aware of is the trees immediately surrounding him.

The trained medical hypnotist can be compared to an observer occupying a helicopter over the forest of life, who has been sitting up there for years observing others go down these respective paths. He knows where they lead and is familiar with what obstacles they present. He can, as an outsider, objectively see patterns of relationship and association not visible to the one involved. He can, via hypnosis, pick up subconscious contents that are in unrecognized conflict with conscious activities. These are the "blips" on the radar screen that reveal to the observer that you are "hiding one thing in your heart, yet uttering another." The experienced medical hypnotist can then, by appropriate suggestion, resolve these conflicts and bring the "inner you" into smooth working harmony with the "outer you."

The objective operator has all the advantages. He is not emotionally involved and can analyze dispassionately. The subjective operator trying to treat himself is trying to placate his own ego ("I am better than everyone else. Nobody can help *me!*") and is in essence fooling himself. Remember the case of the urologist with renal shut-down—his subconscious would not believe his conscious mind. "George" has learned to have very little respect for the conscious mind—probably for very good reasons. It tends to cover up problems rather than digging them up and facing them.

Don't hesitate to ask for help. Don't feel you are inadequate by doing so. All of us need the help of others occasionally. It may be not only shocking to see yourself occasionally as others see you but also very revealing.

Chapter 10

"Faith" Healing

Early in my practice I had discovered multiple fibroid tumors on a patient's uterus as the cause of her enlarged and enlarging abdomen. After the examination was over, I sat down to discuss the treatment for this condition with the lady and her husband. My recommendation in view of the size of the tumors and their steady progressive enlargement was the surgical removal of the uterus with its contained growths (hysterectomy). They smiled politely and said "No, thank you. We'll take care of it ourselves, with God's help."

Upon my questioning their intentions, they told me of their abiding faith in God's ability to heal and that through prayer, now that they knew the nature of the problem, they would correct the problem. They were openly amused at my (then) skeptical attitude and tolerantly agreed to my request to return in six months when, they both assured me, the tumors would be gone. I was convinced that she would be back sooner due to the discomfort of progressive pressure from the growing tumors. I was wrong. Six months later they both politely returned. I re-examined and found to my utter bewilderment a perfectly normal small-sized uterus without any evidence of the previously existing tumors. There had not ever been any doubt in *their* minds as to the ultimate outcome. They returned at my request only.

What made the tumors go away? What does God have to do with it?

It has been pointed out that the inclusion of the study of E.S.P. and parapsychology into academic institutions has been delayed and hampered in the United States by the block of organized religions. They were hesitant because they feared that studies of this nature may serve to undermine religious principles and beliefs. Atheistic materialism in Russia did not serve to block these studies there. It is ironical that the students in Russia are reported to have arrived at a concept of a supreme being through the study of parapsychology, the same route we were afraid would destroy the concept.

What does God have to do with all this? Is there a God? Or, the latest: is God dead? It is not the purpose of this book to presume to be able to discuss such questions from a theological basis. However, we can point out along with the Russian scientists that things don't seem to just happen in conformity with the law of mere chance and that probability curves don't seem to coincide with reality. Things happen not at random but according to patterns and plans with the implication that somebody or something is "running" this marvelous show and that there is meaning and purpose to all life on this planet.

Academic parapsychologists bearing the bruises and scars from previous encounters with religionists are understandably hesitant to be associated with these antagonists. They try to steer clear of simple acceptable terms like "God." And, in their desperate striving for academic recognition they do not want to be associated with any religious bed-fellows. As a result, the simple term "soul" comes out of their verbalistic jungle as the "non-corporeal personal agency."

Can't you just visualize the academic parapsychologist's child going to bed at night saying his prayer: "Now I lay me down to temporary conscious non-awareness. I pray to the non-personal Supreme Intelligence my non-corporeal personal agency to keep."

The Creator as the healer

I do not know where to interject God into the healing process for the simple reason that I don't believe He was ever separate from it. As stated before, there never is God *and anything* but rather God *in everything*. We doctors, as mere humans, can hold flesh to flesh with our sutures, but only the Creator can effect healing. The many mechanisms described previously, and the indirect and direct psychosomatic effects, are but other marvelous non-understood ways in which healing occurs.

There is another category of healing which is even more God-inspired and even less understood under the heading of "faith" healing. Now I am a strong believer in the benefit of prayer. I have seen its beneficial results many times since this one case. Furthermore, I know from experience the more rapid rate of healing, the smoother convalescence in patients who have deep faith in God. They are a joy to the nursing staff and everyone feels uplifted from the privilege of being near them. However, "gullible gussies" will immediately say that all healing should be done entirely by faith alone. That if we are "in attunement" we can ask God to do everything; or that if we are but pure in heart and "in harmony" with Him all things will be done for us, automatically. I consider such concepts to be most presumptuous on our part.

The Creator endowed the cranium with its marvelous brain enclosed to serve in many ways. There are certain fundamental things you are expected to do for yourself by utilizing the good logical functions of your conscious mind. For example, do not ask God, via faith healing, to trim your toe-nails. You can do that for yourself. His entrusting that beautifully complicated material mechanism known as a human body to your care is comparable to your being given a fine automobile; the gift carries with it the assumption that you will have pride enough in the possession to take good care of it and treat it with respect. The analogy with the automobile is not too satisfactory because you can trade it in each year for a new model, but your body has to last all this earthly life before you can exchange it. Therefore, take good care of your body, keep it in good repair, attend to proper maintenance, get regular tune-ups and check-ups.

Not only trim your own nails but bring your body into a good "service station" (doctor's office) for a medical check-up at least once a year—or more often if the engine "knocks." Get that annual chest X-ray that picks up early (and therefore treatable) tuberculosis and lung cancer.

Misuse of faith healing

Misuse of faith healing was illustrated by a misguided, elderly lady patient of mine who had not bothered to go to a doctor for years. She even took foolish pride in this. When she developed a persistent, nagging backache she attended a mass meeting of a popular evangelistic "faith healer" who was currently in town.

Under the hypnotic influence of his soothing voice and the laying-on of his "magic" hands to her afflicted back—she went home in comfort. (One of the most dangerous aspects of hypnosis when foolishly used or in the hands of fools is how well it works!) She slept comfortably that night. However, the lady's back snapped in two as she arose from bed the next morning and, shortly after presenting herself for medical care, she died—of a long standing cancerous growth which had it been picked up early through a routine physical examination, could possible have been cured.

Faith healing properly used

Now I don't want to give the impression I am speaking against faith healing. When properly used by honest and intelligent ministers (as represented by the Spiritual Frontiers Fellowship organization) in conjunction with complete medical treatment it has altered the progression of many an illness. My point is—don't stupidly use this wonderful power to put cotton in your ears to keep from hearing the knock in your engine. Don't keep pouring alcohol into your system while challenging God to cure the resultant cirrhosis of your liver. While we are primarily stressing in this book the importance of the functions of the subconscious mind, we don't want you to lose sight of the functions of the logical, reasoning conscious mind. The two minds were meant to work together, each with its specific role.

The conscious logical mind is also God-given and, I'm sure, given with the full expectation of its being put to use.

As a specialist in obstetrics, my advice was sought a few years ago by a colleague in general practice. He was an earnest, conscientious physician who had been asked to make house calls to sign birth certificates for a particular religious sect that did not believe in doctors being in attendance. His role was merely to affix his signature to the birth certificates, nothing else. He asked for my opinion; he got it. Never! I would insist that they come to the office for proper prenatal care, and to the hospital for the birth of the child. When we use that God-given conscious mind in the application of a bit of logic we see that about 3% of babies simply cannot safely get out of the uterus without medical aid due to complications that inevitably occur, not from disharmony or loss of attunement with God, but from sheer chance. One of the most dangerous of such complications we encounter is placenta previa, where the placenta (after-birth) is so low in location that it is before or in front of the baby. Because it is the lifeline of the baby and contains so many blood vessels of the mother's uterus, there is an awesome risk of fatal hemorrhage, to both the baby and the mother, when labor sets in. This situation is not diagnosed usually until hemorrhage gives the clue as the opening begins to stretch in labor, and immediate Cesarean section is the treatment.

I predicted to my earnest colleague, who did not want to go against the religious beliefs of his patients, even if they go against his medical judgment, that he would not only sign a few birth certificates but would, eventually and inevitably have two death certificates to sign. It took a few years, but my prediction was right. A mother and her baby both died unnecessarily, at home in a pool of blood. The husband resignedly stated, "God took them." I vehemently disagree. Utter stupidity took them! God endowed humans with a logical reasoning conscious mind with the full intention that it be used. Repeatedly taking such chances is like repeatedly playing Russian roulette and is neither God inspired nor God approved.

Common sense with functions of the subconscious

In recognizing the functions of the subconscious don't neglect the good conscious logical mind you were also endowed with. Get your annual medical check-up, annual chest X-ray; don't wait until something hurts to see a doctor or dentist; prevention is preferable to treatment. Don't wait until the radiator freezes up to add preventative antifreeze. Remember, you can't trade this model in on a later one—not in this life span at least.

Power of sincere prayer

Now, back to the process of healing. We have described how the subconscious can affect the rate of healing by direct suggestion (the leg fractures in the armed forces). We have described how direct suggestion in anesthetized patients resulted in better and more rapid healing of surgical cases. What other ways can we affect healing? I personally feel that sincere prayer directed toward healing the afflicted can be effective in three ways: first, by direct psychokinetic power; second, indirectly by telepathy; and third, directly via intercession of the Supreme Being. Let's consider these three categories one at a time.

1. Psychokinetic effect of direct thought action through prayer

If, as has been previously shown, thoughts can affect the rate of growth of plants, can we assume that thought has a similar direct action on animal flesh? Certainly the case of the hypnosis experiment on leg fractures would illustrate that it can. Very little is understood, within the scope of our present limited state of knowledge, about the exact mechanism of healing. For instance, if you should have a piece of your flesh gouged out, the body will gradually grow new flesh to replace the defect. This new flesh grows steadily until the defect is filled in, then it stops growing. How does it know when to stop?

In lower forms of life, (e.g., salamanders, crustacea, etc.) entire appendages such as legs can be lost and the body is capable of re-growing new ones. Any country boy knows that you can cut a worm in two and get two worms. The head end will grow a new tail, and the tail end will grow a new head. What is the mechanism that makes this possible? No one really knows but let's brainstorm here about a concept that has been in existence for many years and is described in Max Freedom Long's book, *The Secret Science Behind Miracles.*[1] This man's many writings about research into ancient magic keeps protruding into our thinking. At this spot it protrudes in the concept of the "shadow body." This is reputed to be an astral duplication of the earthly body which is visible, like the aura, to the visual perception of subliminal awareness (clairvoyants and mediums). It persists after earthly body death as indicated in dotted lines of the diagram on page 81 of the total personal agent and enables other astral entities to see, at will, the person as he existed in bodily form during incarnated life.

This duplication of the earth body is said to also serve as a negative mold or form which serves to allow reformation or healing of missing or deformed parts of the body during earthly life. The new flesh follows the mold or pattern of the always intact

---

[1] Max Freedom Long, *The Secret Science Behind Miracles* (Vista, Calif.: Huna Research Publications, 1948).

shadow body. In lower animals this enables the appendages to grow back again after being lost.

Credence to this concept has been given in several ways. In one experiment, referred to in an article,[2] by the ingenious use of a spectroscope, phantom limbs were seen on a screen. Here is a further case suggesting biological-electromagnetic research challenges. There are also reports of mediums in trance seeing a full limb on a person shortly after amputation, the limb being visible during the phase when the individual "felt" as if the limb was still there. After this "feeling" faded away, so did the shadowy-body limb previously seen by the medium. The "feeling" by the individual and the "vision" by the medium coincided, without the one knowing about the other.

Could this shadow-body negative mold be what limits the growth of flesh in healing? Could this be what guides the regrowth of two new worms from one? Is this "mold" what allows lower forms of life, unrestricted by complicated conscious minds, to utilize corrective healing? Can humans possibly do this? Instantaneous healing has been reported in Kahuna studies and in religious faith healing—deformed limbs suddenly growing to normal forms under the altered awareness of magic rituals or group hypnosis and powerful suggestion. Is this all fakery, all false reports? Are you *sure*?

Could the altered awareness resulting from rituals possibly temporarily dispose of the hampering clouds of conscious overlay in the complicated human being and momentarily allow healing to occur on a level comparable to the less complex animal bodies? Of course this is pure conjecture at our present state of knowledge, but aren't a lot of research possibilities opened up in relation to phantom limbs? Will the shadow-body be demonstrated by biological electro-magnetics of the future? Did the tumors on the lady's uterus shrink and regress until the organ fit its shadow-body mold from the direct effect of concentrated psychokinesis, as the plants were caused to shrink or be stunted?

2. Telepathy and prayer

Let's consider the second possible mechanism of the effect of prayer, that of telepathy. Subconscious minds receive thoughts of

[2]William Perry Bentley, "An Approach To a Theory of Survival of Personality," *The Journal of the American Society for Psychical Research,* Vol. LIX (January 1965) No. 1.

others and at this level tend to act upon the suggestions—as illustrated in the fractured leg experiments with hypnosis. The healing effect of prayer via both psychokinesis and telepathy will be proportionate to the number of people praying, their individual meditative ability (Reverend Loehr classified individual's praying ability by the degree of effect on plant growth), and the amount of time applied—as also demonstrated by experiments on plants. If plant "flesh" can be measurably affected, can animal flesh?

3. Intercession of the Supreme Being

The third effect wherein the special assistance of the Supreme Being is requested I have personal conviction of, but this, like the evidences of survival, cannot be completely isolated from the other possibile effects or from possible coincidence to produce proof to please the academicians.

However, there are many instances that I believe represent just such assistance granted upon request. Direct intervention of the Supreme Being when appealed to for help, for example, would be the sea gulls which appeared to destroy the locusts in the case of the Mormons. Another example cited to me by an elderly gentleman who told how his mother at a prayer meeting years before had received the telepathic intuition that a group of children being sent by a ship to a distant mission field were in serious danger. She interrupted the prayer meeting to insist that everyone's prayers should be directed immediately to ask God's aid for the children. It was found out later that a fire had broken out in the ship at sea and the children were trapped until the wind suddenly changed direction allowing their rescue. The change was sudden, and the new direction was unheard of in that locality: it occurred at the exact time of the prayer meeting.

True disciples of God have learned to depend upon their deep sincere faith that in time of dire need God will intercede and give aid. John Wesley, the founder of the Methodist Church was noted for his practical utilization of such intercession—once when a group was being charged by an angry bull in a field. Instead of running madly away, John calmly knelt in prayer and asked for God's help. He got it. The bull skidded to a stop, lost its anger and meekly walked away.

Prayer can work miracles

Prayer utilized openly and sincerely (does faith part the obstructing clouds of consciousness?) has been known to work many miracles in healing. The group of earnest workers comprising the Spiritual Frontiers Fellowship (800 Custer Ave., Suite 1, Evanston, Ill. 60202) have had many spiritual healings reported by their members.

Healing also can occur inadvertently by suggestion, just as the mother was "put to sleep," inadvertently, by pure oxygen. An example of inadvertent healing, I believe, is cluttering up the courts and the newspapers—the battle about the cancer-healing powers of a substance called "Krebiozen." The originators of the medicine maintain firmly that it cures cancer and have hundreds of devoted followers who are only too willing to testify that their doctors had predicted their demise from cancer, only to have remissions and apparent cures follow the administration of the wonder drug, Krebiozen. Are these people all frauds? Are they all liars? Are their cures just coincidences? (Very doubtful, there are too many of them.) On the other hand, the A.M.A. and the government via the Public Health Department maintains, just as firmly, that Krebiozen is merely a normal constituent of the blood, an essential amino acid. Are the government chemists all making mistakes in their chemical analysis?

Name calling and accusations of misrepresentation are rife and thousands of dollars are being used up in senseless court battles. Yet, not a dime is allotted to research in the power of suggestion. The chemists are right: the substance *is* a harmless normal constituent of blood; but the witnesses for the defense are right too—faith *does* heal! Why don't we quit ignoring the healing powers of faith and use those court cost dollars to more adequately understand *and utilize* the power of the mind and soul to heal the body? Let's have fewer senseless court fights and more religious and psychosomatic research!

If one mother can gracefully and joyfully give birth without medication, why can't others do the same? They can and do. Careful scientific analysis of the emotional and mental factors involved in parturition was followed by recognition of the psychosomatic process involved which, in turn, was followed by practical adaptation and training of other mothers to do likewise. Result—a new, safe, joyful method of unmedicated childbirth, comprehensively including all aspects, mind-body-soul, and utilizing their inter-reactions to achieve in many what was occasionally spontaneously performed by only a few.

Similarly, if a few humans can heal their cancer by suggestion, why isn't the mechanism of healing carefully analyzed then scientifically applied to the many?

Is a science that stubbornly limits itself to the body and blindly ignores the mind and soul a true science or a pseudoscience?

A recent newspaper article described in detail the thousands of dollars of public and private funds being spent to build an allergy-free house for asthmatic children. At great cost it is to eliminate nearly all materials that children are allergic to and is to be air-conditioned with filtered pollen-free air. And, so, are they never to leave their expensive hot-house where they are secluded from society and home? Wouldn't this fortune in funds be more appropriately applied to psychosomatic studies that would enable these children to cope with the world and become useful members of society instead of being sheltered and isolated in such a limited world of their own? If a few people are cured of allergies by application of psychosomatic principles, cannot the mechanism be studied and then applied to the many?

Healing then, is a physical function of flesh but has psychological and spiritual overtones which affect it in many ways. The term "faith healing" is misleading in itself, as there are many instances of successful healing along these lines in which individuals had no *conscious* faith. In fact they were quite skeptical of the possibility, consciously. But we have seen how the subconscious does not necessarily take stock in, or pay heed to, the conscious mind. No matter how firmly the urologist's conscious mind was reassured that the operation showed no cancer, it took hypnosis and awareness on a subconscious level to achieve healing results.

Considering again the diagram of the total personality, the current terrestial conscious mind may not be developed far enough to grasp the possibility of this type of healing, yet the total personality is very cognizant of these powers and may proceed to act regardless of the attitude on the conscious level. This assumes *honest* skepticism on the part of a wholesome, *open* conscious mind. However, a blind, prejudiced or hostile, emotion-laden conscious mind can block even the most capable subconscious forces with a smothering overlay.

Chapter 11

We Are Never Alone

A bachelor friend of ours is a great cat fancier. He had a black cat that was his companion for many years. In the course of time he occupied several different apartments. The cat would run to beg for food whenever he opened the refrigerator door and when hungry, would pace close to the refrigerator and "meow" to be served. However, our friend related that in one apartment where he lived the cat would never go near that particular refrigerator and always kept a healthy distance from it. The cat would not be enticed to come near it even when proffered food. The animal seemed to be very afraid of this area and would lie with his head toward the refrigerator with a fixed and somewhat fascinated stare. The cat's behavior became a source of entertainment. Our friend's guests would amuse themselves by sneaking up on the preoccupied, tense cat and startle the animal. The cat was so intent on the refrigerator that it could be easily taken by surprise and would leap straight up, nearly "jump out of its skin" in terror when distracted.

When he described the animal's peculiar preoccupation with, and dread of, the refrigerator to his landlady, she offered the following explanation. The former tenant of the apartment was a widow who had lived there for years with her husband prior to his death. After she was alone she disposed of her refrigerator and stove and took her meals out. In the recessed area where the refrigerator had stood, she placed a small table with candles and had for years held regular seances at this spot in which she communicated regularly with the spirit of her "departed" husband. Then she too had died.

Astral awareness

Such happenings bring up another function of animal brains which could easily have been included with our original listing in the chapter dealing with animal instinct, but would have been hard to understand at that point in the book. This function could be labeled "astral awareness" and represents instinctual function No. 15. The subconscious animal brain perceives across the barrier between the unobstructed and obstructed universe, between the astral world and the earthly world.

Animals other than human, lacking reasoning, logical, conscious mind, do not know how to accept these "views" and are frightened by the strangeness. They see non-corporeal entities that do not make sounds or carry the usual identifying smells. Such perception is not limited to cats. Dogs are noted for growling and hair standing on end at something they see and their master doesn't. Horses have been known to shy and rear in fright *before* the human rider saw a ghostly figure; or have been known to shy fearfully from a certain area repeatedly, when the conscious-clouded human rider could see nothing there.

Some friends described to us an experience they had illustrating astral awareness in both a dog and the "animal" brain of their little girl, an only child. The little girl, age 2½ years, would play happily in their living room, supposedly alone, but would carry on a one-sided conversation with an unseen friend who always occupied a particular large chair.

The child was puzzled why the parents couldn't see or hear her favorite companion, Uncle Joe, an adult who sat in this chair and kept her company whenever she wished. They, in turn, attributed her "companion" to a vivid imagination until one evening when the husband found a friendly, large stray dog following him and brought the dog home and let him into the house. The dog explored about the house happily wagging its tail until it came before this particular chair occupied by the "imaginary" Uncle Joe. The dog cringed in fright, its tail went down between its legs, it whined piteously and ran, scratching frantically to be let out the door, and disappeared in terror, not to be seen again.

Does our comparison of the animal-like subconscious portion of the human brain to the animal brain hold true here? Can some human beings "see" across this barrier to the astral existence as animals can? Yes, indeed! Again, human instinctual abilities are comparable but covered. Covered with interfering clouds of conscious activity. Some humans are capable of spontaneously parting these clouds (by means of meditation, hypnosis, stress, etc.) and utilizing their subconscious mind activities along channels of astral awareness, just as they use their other perceptual abilities.

The people who seem to be blessed with this gift are called "sensitives" or "mediums." They are said to be "open," unobstructed and receptive to outside influences. It is the same set-up as with telepathy, clairvoyance, precognition, etc.; there is a little of it manifested in all human beings—somewhere in the course of their lives—but a few individuals seem to be blessed with greater abilities. They are more open, more aware, less "blocked" in their subconscious minds' activities. Could it be that they are older souls who have carried this over from previous usage? Again, do the thinner, as yet uncomplicated, conscious minds of children give them more astral awareness than adults as is true with other instincts. Yes! Many lonely children have very seriously described astral playmates. Many an innocent child ("Blessed are the pure in heart for they shall see God") has described to bewildered parents visitations by a grandparent, after the death of the grandparent! A young couple we know described how the family cat jealously and indignantly demands to be let out, with hair on end in irritation or fear, whenever their little toddler son has an astral visitor. They can tell by the action of the cat that their child's "friend" is visiting. The "friend" is called by name and visits regularly—with the child. He is taken for granted—by the child. Imaginary playmate? Then why, if it is only imaginary, does the cat act resentful?

Astral entities and their influence on mortals

Well, here we go again. Let's set up another hypothesis then see how life and facts fit into our theory.

The hypothesis is that astral entities, both the purely astral (no previous incarnations) and those whose total personal agencies include previous earth lives, are aware of and influence incarnated (or reincarnated) occupants of the planet earth. The theory further states that the unobstructed universe encompasses the obstructed; that we are never alone in the strict sense; that astral entities are assigned to watch over each and every individual on earth.

In illustrating the concept that the earthly world is but a fragment of the larger, more encompassing astral world and that there is constant interaction between the two, so that we are never alone, let us first consider the possibility of communication or of the manifestations of such a connection.

We human beings have the tendency to scoff at any *new* concept or idea; first, we label it as fraud, quackery or insanity. Then, only when we're forced to do so will we take a quick little peek at it. If on taking the little peek, we see a thing of great beauty we call it "an all-encompassing myth," because we're afraid it might all collapse in front of us and then we'll be known as a fool for having accepted it. For most of us the new idea has to be something tangible, something that doesn't demand too much imagination for us to see that it will make our immediate world a nicer place to live in, like television and radio. Usually only then are we willing to accept it.

Conversely, the person who is willing to accept anything and everything without intelligent investigation is just as much a fool as the man at the opposite end of the pole who in his blind prejudiced skepticism accepts nothing. The pity is that this state of existence has been going on for eons of time, and we don't seem to learn from our mistakes. Derisive laughter went up when it was first proposed that the earth was round. Jeers and taunts came with the first telescope and angry accusations of trickery when the first cylindrical record was played. Great courage and fortitude are needed to try to make the world a better place with such odds as this.

If only we all could learn to take the middle path in our efforts to learn about the world, to say "Well, I honestly don't know, but tell me about it and if it sounds sensible I'll think on it!" Even when we try to keep an open mind, an experience generally has to happen to us before we're convinced.

I had an adored grandmother and, in looking back, I'm not sure why I adored her so, for I was more than a little in awe of her. She was a little Kansas farm wife and yet, to me, she always seemed majestic and regal. I can't ever remember her kissing or fondling me as some grandmothers are wont to do, but with one word of approval from her, nothing could dim my spirit for days.

In analyzing this relationship many years later, I came to understand that for me she was a beautiful harbor of security.

She personified kindness and justice and radiated an inner strength I've seldom seen since. You knew that she knew. She knew who she was and why she was here. Blind faith had nothing to do with it. She lived until she was eighty-nine and two days before she was due to leave her little crippled body, she looked up from her sick-bed and said in surprise, "Why Albert, and Otis! How wonderful to have you come."

Albert and Otis were the husband and son she had lost many, many years ago. I had very seldom heard her speak of them; when she did it was with the utmost gentleness and tenderness. Prior to this it had never occurred to me that after death there might be the kind of life in which a spirit kept an identifiable personality or that it was possible for a spirit to see or be seen by those still on earth. I was convinced on that day and remain so to this day that if my grandmother saw it this way, that is the way it was.

Through the many years since my grandmother's death I've heard of many other cases in which the one who is preparing to depart sees and hears those who have preceded them. Some change evidently takes place within the physical body that enables for a short time those who are in the process of crossing the bridge to see what is taking place on either side. These same people in all likelihood have never had a psychic experience before in their lives and probably never would have had if they had continued to live.

That some people never in their lives have a psychic experience does not preclude the fact that other lives are filled with them. Some have them from earliest childhood, some not until later in life, and they have them in various forms and degrees. There are those who find it necessary to go into trance, while others do not.

Methods of communication

Some mediums depend on accoutrements such as an Ouija board, a planchette, a crystal ball, cards or automatic writing, as aids to mental concentration to achieve open receptivity of mind. Others see and hear directly as if they were talking to another person still on the earth plane. All of them soon learn to tell the difference between good and evil spirits and how to protect themselves from undesirable influences. Every true medium I know is a religious person in the deepest meaning of the term.

There are those mediums who have what are called "controls": persons who have graduated into the unobstructed universe and serve as go-betweens. It sometimes happens that the control is attracted to the medium because they had once been close friends on earth; others are attracted because the vibrations are compatible and they work well together. The former is the case with Arthur Ford and his control, "Fletcher."

In the case of Edgar Cayce's mediumship no control as such was used. He obtained his information, he said, by reading the "Akashic records."

Even the very best of mediums never claim one hundred percent accuracy. Mr. Ford, as I remember, is said to be about eighty-five percent accurate, but in our own experiences with him we found his accuracy even higher.

Our experience with a medium

In our determination to leave no stone unturned, we followed the suggestion of a like-minded friend and contacted a local man who our friend said was just in the process of developing as a first rate medium. She felt he held much promise and would go far due to two things: his sincerity and his wholesomeness.

That we acted upon our friend's suggestion and called Jack Young, we have never had cause to regret. We have now been meeting every other Sunday night for two years, and these occasions stand out as bright, fulfilling areas in our lives.

Jack is a sincere, dedicated and sensitive man firmly convinced in his own mind where he stands in relationship to his fellow man and his God. When he conducts a sitting he makes very few requirements, but those he does make must be rigidly adhered to. He steadfastly maintains that you must approach this with the same attitude that you would a regular church service. We have been to many church services but very seldom have we heard sermons of the same high degree of spiritual quality that we often get on these evenings when Jack goes into trance. When this takes place his whole personality, his voice, his approach and, to some degree, his vocabulary undergo a radical change.

Should you think this is just a way for him to expound on his pet theories rather than that he is a true channel, all you have to do is listen and observe. He will walk into the room, meet our friends or relatives about whom he knows nothing and sympathetically say to someone "I'm so sorry. You have just shed tears." This was the case with Bob's sister who had just lost her husband, and with a distinguished looking gentleman and his wife who were completely unknown to any of us, and arrived with other invited friends. The gentleman was a complete skeptic and had come only to please his wife and our friends who brought them. It was amusing to see Jack walk by this gentleman, stop abruptly, turn and say "What's this with you and an airplane that was used as a getaway by some bank robbers many, many years ago?" It was most rewarding to see the look of absolute astonishment on the man's face as he said, "Why yes, how did you know that?" And so it goes all through the evening, every evening that we meet. One of the most incredible things he did was his psychometric reading when a guest handed him the diary of his incurably ill wife. Jack felt of it a moment then proceeded to describe the woman, after first saying it was a woman, told of her personality, her European place of birth, the degenerate state of her health and ended by saying that he saw a wedding ring about to be taken off. In another six months this proved to be true, as her terrible suffering of seventeen years' duration came to a merciful end.

The method by which Jack receives all this information varies. Sometimes he is awake and alert, sometimes in trance. I'm sure some of it is telepathy and clairvoyance, but then there are times when he seems to be in actual conversation with a person or persons unseen. Quite often when he is being impressed by someone who wants to be acknowledged, to tell their story he will actually suffer the pains they suffered as they crossed over. Such was the case one night when he had only arrived, entered the room where several people were, suddenly grabbed his head, moaned and was obviously in great pain. The pain seemed to increase in its intensity until he finally called out and said, "Who here lost a young man with a severe head injury." A lovely white-headed lady whom we had just met acknowledged that she had. She proceeded to tell us the story of how her youngest son, then nineteen, had been in the service and one day while changing a tire on a bomber trailer had met his death as the rim on the huge tire he was changing flew off due to the great pressure in the tire, caught him just above the eyes and nearly decapitated him. Jack then went on to give a most beautiful and reassuring message to the mother from the boy, some very personal things that none of us could have known.

The chandelier in our library where we hold our meetings is on a rheostat which is turned very low. It often happens that as Jack greets and announces the arrival of some unseen guest the lights will flare up and dim down. Some evenings they are extremely active, other times not quite so much so or very little. At the beginning we thought there was probably some other answer for this but have checked it out with household currents as they are related to appliances and have found nothing. We have even spent hours sitting in the room when Jack was not there, but under the same conditions and could not achieve a single flicker.

Among our acquaintances, especially the professional ones, there are those who find it incredible that we can believe in survival and/or the communication of spirits. It is at such times I like to refer them to Socrates' *Apology* wherein he states: "Did ever man, Meletus, believe in the existence of human things, and not of human beings? Did ever any man believe in horsemanship, and not in horses? or in flute playing and not in flute players? No, my friend, there is no man who ever did. But now please to answer the next question: Can a man believe in spiritual and divine agencies, and not in spirits or demigods? He cannot."

It is not that I think, that because Socrates believed it, it is any more or less so. It is only that there are those who find what I think to be of absolutely no consequence, and I find that if you can quote someone like Socrates, they are most terribly impressed!

We have another friend, a Mr. Harry Byers, who works with a medium in another state whose percentage of accuracy is so great that when he started describing some activity by an enemy country in our coastal waters, everyone became very excited. Our friend felt it his duty as a good citizen to relay this information to authorities but was hardly prepared for the attention it received and the arrival of government officials who wondered how this classified information had leaked out. We were then all upset because we felt it must surely have some basis in truth. Several months later this was verified by headlines in our daily papers.

There is enough good material in Harry's work with this medium to make a very interesting book; there are often amusing little side lights especially when you're working with someone who is not oriented to this way of thinking. One that happened to Harry took place on the night they had an appointment at a professor's house in another city. Both Harry and the medium were most anxious to have this man work with them and wanted very much to make a favorable impression on him, since they were fully aware that he thought the whole subject, including them, a little on the strange side. Since the medium lived in an isolated part of his state, he kept and flew his own plane and did almost all his travelling this way. This particular day was no exception. When Harry arrived in the city he located the professor's house where they had agreed to meet, knocked at the door and said "I'm Harry Byers. Could you tell me if my friend, Jim Thompson, has arrived as yet?" He had no more said this and the professor was just starting to say "No,—" than Harry heard the sound of an airplane overhead, looked up, recognized its markings and said "Oh no, there he is now!" With that the professor, not knowing he was expected by plane, looked up toward the ceiling with a wild look on his face and said, "Where! Where!" He seemed rather undone for the rest of the evening.

It has happened many times over that one stumbles into this field by playing what many people think is just a game, since Ouija boards can be found on most game counters in any average department store. These people sometimes find out the hard way how very dangerous this can become. If a person is too open to psychic influences, or too gullible and takes everything that comes as if it were a message from the Arch-angel Gabriel, direct from the Holy of Holies, this can play havoc with his life.

Warnings are repeatedly given by advanced mediums as to the inherent dangers in this whole field. They frown heavily on the use of the Ouija board and the planchette because evil or mischievous entities cannot be filtered out as readily as they can by the more direct means of communication. A medium who is being directly influenced picks up the emotional conditions of the person communicating and can easily tell by the resulting emotions within himself about the goodness or sadness or illness of the communicant.

A medium is a very sensitive instrument who can by choice put aside his own ego, tune in and put himself at the service of a will not his own. This other will can belong to another entity on either the earth plane or any one of the astral planes. In the living it is subconscious and supernormal; in the departed ones it is conscious and normal. When this action is manifested through the living it is called animistic and when it is through the so-called dead it falls into the category of spiritistic phenomena.

Over the years, in observing many mediums we have been

impressed by the honest confusion on their part when pressed as to whether the entity being presented is on earth or is deceased. They strive to determine this but it is obvious that they sometimes just cannot tell the difference; they don't know and say so. It is significant that the subconscious mind of the earth-living human appears identical to the total mind of the deceased person. It is also significant in considering fakery or imagination on the part of the medium, that they obviously are confused and honestly cannot tell the difference in some instances.

Various degrees of mediumship

It has been said before that there are all degrees of mediumship: some see only to the extent that they can sense an oncoming danger to themselves, some can see or hear paranormal things in a moment of crisis, there are those who have dream warnings, while others have such broad psychic openings they can communicate at will with advanced souls and thereby receive beautiful, inspiring and very illuminating messages.

A great skeptic will say, "Of course they're beautiful, but it's only a thought from the medium's own mind." In any one particular case he might be right. However, the one thing that has turned us into such staunch believers is the fact that in all the hundreds of books we have read on this subject the story is always the same; no matter what century it was written in, no matter from what part of the world it came, regardless of the sex or the degree of education of the communicator, *the story is the same.* Yet we cannot say that about the seventy-seven (by actual count) different religious denominations in our own town, in our own time: *Their stories are not the same.*

The case of Daisy Driden

Even when the story comes from the mouth of babes, it is still the same. One of the most beautiful examples of this I have ever heard of comes from a book written in Italian by Ernesto Bozzano and titled *Discarnate Influences In Human Life.* In this book he tells a story about a little ten-year-old girl named Daisy Driden, a story which we feel is not only touching but extremely significant. We shall reproduce the story here, complete with comments on the case as described in the original work by Stanley De Brath, taken from Bozzano's book:[1]

Daisy Driden

This story is taken from the *Journal of the American A.P.R.* (1918, p. 375). It is a touching episode of a sick girl who in the last three days of her life sees and converses with a deceased younger brother and other spirit entities, while seeing transient visions of the Beyond. As the case fills seventeen pages of the review, I must limit myself to a few essential extracts.

The girl's father was the Reverend David Anderson Driden, a Methodist missionary. He and his wife took note of what the girl said during the last days of her life. After his wife's death, her notes were published in a pamphlet, in the hope of bringing comfort to some doubting and suffering soul.

The girl's name was Daisy. She was born in Marysville, California, on September 9th, 1854. She was therefore just ten years old.

The Reverend F. J. Higgings, in his introduction to the pamphlet, observes:

Instances of the opening of the spiritual senses just before death are by no means unheard of.... But such experiences are usually brief, and consequently convey to those around no definite knowledge of the other world, even when names of departed ones are called and words descriptive of them spoken. That which was remarkable in Daisy's case of open vision was its unusual length and the clearness of her revelations, resulting from the fact that there was time for her to familiarize herself with the wonderful things she saw and heard.

...She died of enteritis following on typhoid fever, from which she seemed to be recovering during the two weeks before her death, but she steadily maintained that her departure was near. Four days before her death enteritis set in, and for the first twenty-four hours she suffered greatly. After that the pain passed and she became clairvoyant. This was noticed first by reason of a text from the Gospel of St. John read to her by her father, which led her to remark that she hoped to return to console her parents. She added: "I'll ask Allie about it."

Allie was her brother who had died of scarlet fever, aged six, about seven months before. She waited a short time and then said: "Allie says I may go to you sometimes; he says it is possible, but you will not know when I am there. But I can speak to your thought."

[1]Ernesto Bozzano, *Discarnate Influences In Human Life* (London International Institute for Psychical Research). n.d.

The mother writes:

As I have said, Daisy lingered on for three days after the first agonizing twenty-four hours had passed.... During this time she lived in both worlds, as she expressed it. Two days before she left us the Sunday School superintendent came to see her. She talked very freely about going, and sent a message by him to the Sunday School. When he was about to leave, he said: "Well, Daisy, you will soon be over the dark river." After he had gone, she asked her father to explain what he meant by "The dark river." He tried to explain it, but she said: "It is all a mistake; there is no river; there is no curtain; there is not even a line that separates this life from the other life." And she stretched out her little hands from the bed, and with a gesture said: "It is here and it is there. I know it is so, for I can see you all, and I see them there at the same time." We asked her to tell us something of that other world and how it looked to her, but she said: "I cannot describe it; it is so different, I could not make you understand..."

I was then sitting by her bedside, her hand clasped in mine. Looking up so wistfully to me, she said: "Dear Mama, I do wish you could see Allie; he is standing beside you." Involuntarily I looked around, but Daisy thereupon continued: "He says you cannot see him because your spirit eyes are closed, but that I can, because my body only holds my spirit, as it were, by a thread of life." I then inquired: "Does he say that now?" "Yes, just now," she answered. Then wondering how she could be conversing with her brother, when I saw not the least sign of conversation, I said: "Daisy, how do you speak to Allie? I do not hear you nor see your lips move." She smilingly replied: "We just talk with our think...." I then asked her further: "Daisy, how does Allie appear to you? Does he seem to wear clothes?" She answered: "Oh, no, not clothes such as we wear. There seems to be about him a white, beautiful something, so fine and thin and glistening, and oh, so white, and yet there is not a fold, or a sign of thread in it, so it cannot be cloth. But it makes him look so lovely." Her father then quoted from the Psalmist: "He is clothed with light as a garment." "Oh, yes, that's it." She replied.

During those last days of illness Daisy loved to listen to her sister Lulu as she sang for her, mostly from the Sunday School song-book, and after one of these hymns, which spoke of the angels and their "snowy wings," Daisy exclaimed: "Lulu, isn't it strange? We always thought the angels had wings! But it is a mistake; they don't have" and Lulu replied; "But they must have wings, else how could they fly down from heaven?" "Oh, but they don't fly." she answered, "they just come. When I think of Allie, he is here."

Once I inquired: "How do you see the angels?" She replied: "I do not see them all the time; but when I do, the walls seem to go away, and I can see ever so far, and you couldn't begin to count the people; some are near, and I know them; others I have never seen before...."

The morning of the day she died she asked me to let her have a small mirror. I hesitated, thinking the sight of her emaciated face would be a shock to her. But her father, sitting by her, remarked: "Let her look at her poor little face if she wants to." So I gave it to her. Taking the glass in her two hands, she looked at her image for a time, calmly and sadly. At length she said: "This body of mine is about worn out. It is like that old dress of Mamma's hanging there in the closet. She doesn't wear it any more, and I won't wear my body any more, because I have a new spiritual body which will take its place. Indeed, I have it now, for it is with my spiritual eyes I see the heavenly world while my body is still here. You will lay my body in a grave because I will not need it again. It was made for my life here, and now my life here is at an end, and this poor body will be laid away, and I shall have a beautiful body like Allie's. Do not cry, Mamma. It is better for me to go now. I might have grown up to be a wicked woman, like so many do. God knew what was best for me...." Then she said to me: "Mamma, open the shutters and let me look out at the world for the last time. Before another morning I shall be gone." As I obeyed her loving request, she said to her father: "Raise me up, Papa." Then, supported by her father, she looked through the window whose shutters I had opened, and called out: "Good-bye sky. Good-bye trees. Good-bye flowers. Good-bye white rose. Good-bye, red rose. Good-bye beautiful world," and added: "How I love it, but I do not wish to stay."

That evening when it was half-past eight, she herself, observed the time, and remarked: "It is half-past eight now; when it is half-past eleven, Allie will come for me." She was then for the time being reclining on her father's breast with her head upon his shoulder. This was a favourite position, as it rested her. She said: "Papa, I want to die here. When the time comes, I will tell you."

Lulu had been singing for her and as half-past eight was Lulu's bedtime, she arose to go. Bending over Daisy, as she always did, she kissed her, and said: "Good night." Daisy put up her hand and, stroking tenderly her sister's face, said to her: "Good night." When Lulu was half-way up the stairs, Daisy again called out after her, in clear, sweet, earnest tones: "Good night and good-bye, my sweet, darling Lulu."

At about a quarter-past eleven she said: "Now, Papa, take me up; Allie has come for me." After her father had taken her, she asked us to sing. Presently someone said:

"Call Lulu," but Daisy answered promptly: "Don't disturb her, she is asleep," and then, just as the hands of the clock pointed to the half-hour past eleven, the time she had predicted that Allie was to come to take her with him, she lifted up both arms and said: "Come, Allie," and breathed no more. Then tenderly laying her loved but lifeless form upon the pillow, her father said: "The dear child has gone," and added: "She will suffer no more."

There was a solemn stillness in the room. We could not weep, and why should we? We could only thank our Heavenly Father for the teachings of her last days, those days rendered sacred by the glory of heaven which illumined one. We felt that the room must be full of angels come to comfort us, for a sweet peace fell upon our spirits, as if they had said: "She is not here, she has risen."

(Professor Hyslop wrote to the sister of the clairvoyant, Miss Lulu Driden, who confirmed the scrupulous exactitude of the facts described in her mother's diary, and gave him permission to publish them in his review.)

The amazing clairvoyant powers of Daisy Driden

Here I must end my citations, with regret that I cannot reproduce the whole account. In this episode, besides the fact of the unusual prolongation of the supernormal visions, with complete absence of delirium until the last moment, we must note the other fact that the observations of the clairvoyant about the spiritual world agree admirably with the spiritualistic doctrine, and all this through the agency of a child absolutely ignorant of the existence of this doctrine.

Who suggested them to her? Certainly not the parents by telepathic thought transmissions, since they were as ignorant as their daughter concerning spiritualistic doctrines, which in 1864 were hardly in bud. How then could she conceive for herself so many transcendental truths diametrically opposed to those learned from the religion of her fathers? How could she formulate spontaneously such profound ideas as those implied in the statement that the spiritual and terrestrial worlds interpenetrate: "It is here, and it is there?" That "there is not even a line to separate this life from the other life?" That the spirits speak to each other by thought? That they perceive telepathically the thought addressed to them by the living and come instantaneously and independently of any limits of distance? That spirits do not fly but transport themselves?

That only she could see her little dead brother, because at that moment she was only united to the world of the living by a single, weak thread of life? That the dead return to visit their dear ones, but that their presence is for the most part not perceived, although they converse with their thought (or their subconscious)? That man possesses a "spiritual body" imminent in the physical body? That the spiritual world is so different from ours as to be impossible to describe, because it would be impossible to make oneself understood? And what a profound intuition of the truth lies in the observation: "Do not cry, Mamma, it is much better for me to go now. ... God knew what was best for me." Let us admit frankly: the hallucinatory, autosuggestive and telepathic hypotheses do not enter into all this. It follows that the visions of the child Daisy cannot be explained except by admitting that the clairvoyant founded her observations on facts in some manner objective, and furnished explanations suggested to her by others; as she herself affirmed.

How curious in this connection are the dialectical efforts of the Reverend F. J. Higgings to distinguish the phenomena that occurred at the death-bed of the child Daisy Driden from those of modern Spiritualism, for the purpose of demonstrating how only the first are comfortable with the sayings in the Holy Bible, and that therefore they only should be considered as divine revelations! He observes:

> She was in no sense a spiritual medium, any more than were Moses or St. John, who wrote the book of Revelation. No spirit took possession of her even for an instant, or spoke through her. But with her spiritual sight and hearing opened by the Lord Himself, she was, during those last three days, simply a spectator of the beings and objects in the spiritual world, while remaining bodily in this, owing to the fact, as the doctor said, that she was really three days dying.

It is unnecessary to remark that Mr. Higgings' observations only show his scanty knowledge of spiritualistic doctrines. The truth of the matter is this: if we eliminate the hallucinatory hypothesis, then the child Daisy's visions are strictly and classically spiritualistic.

Mr. Stanley De Brath, in his book, *Psychic Research* (page 141), cites the case of Daisy Driden and observes:

> For my own part, this simple and most touching narrative

is more evidential to me than all the disquisitions of philosophies and the doctrines of divines. I do not envy those who can
read it unmoved and fail to see, independently of the obvious
honesty of the mother's account, the internal evidences of the
child's real and actual sight, contradicting the accustomed
imagery of winged angels, her recognition of her brother, her
description of children unknown to her then 'grown up,' her
rejection of the 'river' and the 'city'; all so absolutely concor-
dant with what we have from other sources. Let those who can
speak of this child's perceptions as 'hallucinations' and 'phan-
tasms' keep their cheerless and blind opinions if they will. It is
they who are the victims of illusion. If this case stood alone
there might be some excuse for doubt; but it does not stand
alone. There are many other similar visions by dying children
whose unsophisticated evidence is worth all the skeptical specu-
lation with which the literature of the subject is encumbered.

So says De Brath, and I think that a majority of readers will
think as he does.

Significance of Daisy Driden's story

Daisy's beautiful little story illustrates how completely "una-
lone" we are. She not only saw her little brother; she saw
playmates grown-up; she saw wing-less angels and probably a host
of other familiar and unfamiliar beings. The point to be made here
is that Daisy never had been alone any more than any of us ever
are.

This point that we are never truly alone, that loved ones who
loved us during earthly life are just as interested in us and are even
more aware of our problems after passing on to astral existence
was well illustrated by an experience told me by a lady in the
audience after a lecture.

Her son was serving in the Viet-Nam conflict. She had
awakened from sleep just two months earlier, crying out for help.
She had vividly seen her son fall wounded in the field. She had
struggled to leave where she was to go to him but could not do it;
she seemed bound down. However, she saw his younger brother go
to him and remain by his side giving solace. This younger brother
had died many years before, but she saw him clearly and distinctly, and he was as free to move about as she was restrained.
The wounded older brother recovered from his wounds and
returned to verify his mother's clairvoyant dream as to time,

location of wound, and hearing the soothing words of his long
dead brother.

An astral entity helps prevent a suicide

Another illustration of astral entities being interested in and
helping incarnated occupants of this planet earth was evident in
the case of one of our young mothers. I had presided at the birth
of the three children of this young lady and all was well. At least
all was well until I unexpectly got a call from the emergency room
one night with the startling message that she had tried to commit
suicide with an overdose of sleeping pills.

My records showed no mention of depression and I was at a
loss to understand her sudden attempt on her own life and
considerably chagrined at my own medical inadequacy for not
having foreseen her problem; after all, I had been her physician for
three children's births.

After her stomach was pumped and she was physically
restored, I referred her to a psychiatrist for treatment. Following
his work up he promptly referred her back to me with a mischievous twinkle in his eye, "This is more in your province, Bob."

I have not tried to hide my convictions from my col-
leagues—quite the contrary—and as a result take considerable
good natured kidding and some not so good natured as well. I
have a healthy disrespect for some physicians who may even be
members of psychic research groups but who furtively skulk about
for fear someone may discern this "blight" on their status. The
light of spiritual awareness should not be hidden under a bushel. If
there is any reality to religious freedom in this democracy, why
should *anyone* and particularly physicians try to hide their interests and beliefs? I have never turned down an invitation to speak
publicly on this subject and feel my status has been thereby
elevated in the minds of the thinking public, not lowered as some
seem to fear.

I didn't understand what my psychiatrist friend was talking
about until I studied this woman's case. It seems she "heard
voices" speaking to her following a severe emotional jolt when she
discovered her husband was not true to her. Anyone who hears
voices is losing his mind—or so her conscious mind "reasoned," so
she felt suicide was the only path left.

Age-regressing her under hypnosis to get the total picture of her personality, I discovered that she had been born out of wedlock, abandoned at birth never to know her true mother. She had been reared in an orphan's home for the first eight years then adopted by an elderly farm couple who were barren and childless.

I am repeatedly shocked by man's inhumanity to man. This elderly couple only wanted a worker, not a child to love. She was a veritable slave who was forced to perform nearly continuous labor. She was extremely lonely and had no playmates, no neighbors; it was an isolated, barren countryside. On the few occasions when she was momentarily free she would retreat to the seclusion of an empty irrigation canal near the farm. Here she was regularly joined by spirit people who served as playmates and kept her company. They would talk to her joyfully and cheer her in her loneliness.

A few years later she ran away from this oppressive situation and things went well for her. She fell in love, married, bore her children and in her happiness had long forgotten (consciously) about her childhood mystical companions.

Then came the shock of her husband's unfaithfulness. In her distress she retreated to solitude and the old feeling of rejection, of being unloved and lonely, as in her early childhood, overwhelmed her. Her ever present spirit companions tried to cheer her again, as they had in her youth. However, she had consciously forgotten them after these many years and thought she was losing her mind. Sane people don't hear voices when no one is there!

After some indoctrination into awareness and acceptance of the phenomenon of clairaudience and an invitation to join our regular seance group, this mother has adjusted well to her problems. Blessed people hear voices. The psychiatrist was right: this was more in our province. Of course there are hallucinated "voices" in cases of true schizophrenia where contact with reality is actually lost. However, I wonder how many other cases of similar nature may have gone unrecognized?

The blessings of psychic help

How foolish of us to think that while we're on-stage in this fabulous extravaganza called "Life" that we're the whole show! Patterns are repeated in all phases of existence throughout the Universe, and so it is in this. There is the all-important director who cast you in the part in the first place, who also decided on the play you were going to be in and who your co-actors were going to be; then there is the most valued member of the team, your guardian angel or guide, who serves as your prompter should you forget your lines or get off on the wrong path. There are all the technicians who work backstage that help to make your present production the success or the failure that it is.

No matter how great the success may be it is a wise actor or actress who remembers while standing "stage center" with the spotlights playing about him and with the glorious sound of applause ringing in his ears, that he could not have done all this alone. It is very important to the people standing in the wings watching your performance to know that you haven't forgotten for one minute that they're all still there wishing the best for you and cheering you on.

Chapter 12

Spirit Manifestations
We Have Known

There are a host of things to be listed under types of manifestations, all of them important and none to be ignored or taken lightly. Probably no one person has been involved in his own personal experiences, in the whole of the list, and this seems to apply to professional mediums as well as the average person. No one has been able to give me answers for why a particular set of things happen to one person and not another, or why you have no choice nor even a voice in the matter. All I know is that when a particular thing does happen to *you* everything else pales by comparison.

Are ghosts real?

Lest we give the impression that we are quite unique in that spirits manifest themselves in our lives at Bradmar, let us quote from a newspaper. We are blessed, but far from unique in these occurrences. Probably prompted by the trivia of Halloween a local newspaper, *The Denver Post,* Saturday, October 30, 1965 carried the following front page banner in large type: "Are Ghosts Real? Of Course, Says Jesuit Scholar—." The article this referred to appeared in the Religion Section, was written by George Cornell and said in part:

> But really now, in this intensely scientific age, are there actually such things as spooks, ghosts and poltergeists?

Of course there are, says the Reverend Terence M. Petry, a Jesuit scholar. "I certainly believe in ghosts, though I have never seen one. I find the evidence for them overwhelming."

Father Petry, who has gathered records on the phenomenon and had extensive first-hand experience with it himself, says "ghosts and kindred spirits seem to be very out of place in this busy world."

But nevertheless, he insists, they exist, and he has had numerous encounters with one species of them   poltergeists, which means literally "a ghost who pelts things."

"A mountain of evidence supports the existence of preternatural beings and goes under this name," he writes in the Catholic magazine, *America*.

Numerous groups, learned and otherwise, carry on research into such manifestations. Duke University has a continuing program of analysis of occult and psychical happenings, and a growing file of records.

Father Petry, an Englishman and presently editor of the *Catholic Standard* in British Guiana, says that the United States doesn't seem to have as many ghosts as older European cultures.

The reason, he suggest, may be that ghosts seem to prefer old houses and Americans have a "habit of pulling houses down as soon as they are 40 years old."

But there may soon be a resurgence of ghosts in America," he adds, "since most historical figures seem to start making their midnight appearances about 200 years after death."

The United States is getting close to that age, and already has reached it, in regard to the Colonial period. Noted figures in a country's history seem to be most common in reports of reappearances.

One theory, Father Petry says, is that "Just as we see stars that may long ago have ceased to exist, so a ghostly apparition may be coming from a human entity once endowed with unusual radioactivity which left vibrations on the ether that persons living now can somehow sense...."

Although English householders treasure "a genuine ghost," he says, "Americans seem to find a family ghost almost as undesirable as a family skeleton, and they tend to keep quiet about mysterious goings-on at the midnight hour."

Let us reassure Father Petry that: our beloved Bradmar home is now 45 years old; that it will not be torn down; that it is English in more ways than design and composition in that the occupants similarly treasure a genuine ghost; that we have no fear of the dead but that we have a great fear of the (steadily fewer) ignorant living who will not face facts and who persist in persecuting those who do; and, as evidenced by this book and especially this chapter that here are some Americans who have no tendency to keep quiet about goings-on in their home just because they appear mysterious to others.

Some people will say that all this is a matter of faith, that you *want* to believe in all of these phenomena. Sometimes I think what they really want to say is that the believers are being very gullible. Suffice it to say that, in my case, I at least have polite friends. It is very true that for years I had been looking for answers, but it had never occurred to me to look in this area; they came to us unasked and unsought prior to our interest and study which followed as a consequence. I have sometimes wondered whether perhaps the reason they did was that we were in a position to help others who considered themselves to have similar problems. They viewed the occurrences as problems since they didn't understand what was happening to them and as a result had become frightened. Dr. Bradley has had many patients come to his office and to our home who were seeking answers to some or all of these questions. It is most gratifying to see fear and tension drain from their faces when they are reassured that they are not losing their minds just because they have heard or seen something unexplainable.

Help has been given not only to those who come as patients but also to the general public who go to hear his many public talks on this subject. Here again it would seem that all of this has been taken out of our hands, (if indeed it was ever in them) and arranged as a job for us to do.

A job to do

Giving public talks on this subject all started one day when Dr. Bradley, who was the president of a men's service club at the time, was faced with the problem of his speaker becoming ill and being forced to cancel the scheduled talk. Since it was a very last minute development there wasn't time to find a substitute speaker, so he decided to give the program himself.

As fate would have it we had just returned from a four day meeting in Chicago, held by the Spiritual Frontiers Fellowship of which we are members. It was our first meeting and we had been very reassured and inspired by all we had seen and heard during those days. Evidently Dr. Bradley had been able to transfer some of this to his audience that day for the talk was a great success.

Requests for this same kind of talk on E.S.P. and related subjects have been coming in ever since then.

The giving of these talks in themselves has led to some interesting experiences. Dr. Bradley never fails to come home without some fascinating stories told to him by others or something he has experienced himself. Some of these stories will be shared with you in this book but they represent a very small part of the whole. The people in his audiences find it such a relief to be able to talk to someone about their experiences; even though they may have had only one in their lives, it is important to them. One of the things that has happened to Bob himself, is that, when the question and answer period comes, he finds himself giving answers he didn't know he knew, sensible and beautiful answers. These come without conscious mind processing and are obviously from a subconscious level.

The average well-balanced person has perhaps some time in his life seen fraud or had an experience in this area that has been particularly repellent to him and justifiably so. I know we have. We have seen fraud in its most perfected form. As disgusted as I was at the time, I am now grateful for those experiences since they give us a basis for comparison and make one's gratitude and appreciation for the honest people in this field so much greater.

With your own experiences in your own home with no one around but your own family, and even some of those skeptical, it doesn't leave you with any other choice but to believe what you see, especially when it is a physical phenomenon. When you see lights going off and on, appliances starting to run, and the sprinkling system begin to function, all without any visible means, it certainly makes you pause to consider things that may never before have occurred to you. We have spent the better part of the last few years delving into the whole field, carefully considering and sifting and weighing and analyzing. None of our concepts have been idly arrived at.

Some interesting little experiences

Of all the many things that have happened to us, not one has been frightening or harmful. Some even seem to be done with an almost tongue-in-cheek attitude. The first of these was aboard an airliner on a trip to New York. Since there were just the three of us, Sieg, Bob and myself, we decided to sit abreast so that we might share our books and conversation. When the hostess served us our lunches I tucked the books away and placed my purse on the floor between my feet. After lunch Bob reached across me and handed Sieg a medicated toothpick his dentist had recommended for such occasions. As we continued chatting away, I idly noticed that Sieg in his fiddling with the wooden toothpick had snapped it in two. A little more time was spent exchanging thoughts and impressions before we went back to our books.

As I reached for the book I had been reading, I also picked up my purse thinking a cigarette would be nice. When I opened my purse I was startled to see nested down in some tissue the very same medicated toothpick Sieg had been fooling with a short time before. I know it was the same one; it was snapped in two just as he had snapped his. Bob still had his in his hand and I had not used one nor have I ever used one, so there was no likelihood that I would have had one in my purse.

"Why" such a bit of whimsy as the toothpick should take place I've no idea, any more than there seems to be any reason "why" for various other things. Quite late one night as I was preparing for bed, I was suddenly riveted to the spot by a tremendous sound, that even though I could place it as having come from outside the window, still filled the whole room. The nearest thing I can liken it to would be the sound of a great Chinese gong. No more had the first sounds died away than it happened again. The only thing I could think of was that the children had dragged home something, but I thought they must surely have lost their minds to be making such a noise at that time of night. I went rushing downstairs full of indignation and fury only to find everything dark except for one bathroom light. As I went tearing down the hall shouting "What in the name of heaven are you doing!" a very sheepish Sieg came out and said meekly, "Brushing my teeth." Needless to say I felt pretty foolish. It took a great deal of talking on my part to make him even begin to understand what I was running around shouting about.

One of the most peculiar things ever to happen to me occurred one night as the whole family was dining at our favorite Mexican restaurant. We were seated at a long narrow table, I at one end and my eldest son opposite me; we were happily engaged in some very animated conversation when I was suddenly jolted with the sensation of cold water on my legs. Imagine my surprise when I discovered that it *was* cold water. I looked at the table, saw that nothing had spilled. The tablecloth was dry. It occurred to me that perhaps someone had spilled something earlier and it was just now seeping through. We looked under the table, felt of the table but could find nothing that gave the slightest clue where the water had come from.

Two months later Sieg and I were out shopping and just as we were entering the big double doors of one of our busiest stores, I gasped with surprise as I again felt the sensation of cold water being thrown on my legs. The first thing that occurred to me was that there was a window washer up on the building and we had gotten in the way of some spilled water. It was quite a surprise to look up and not see a window washer or even any windows. I noticed that neither Sieg nor any of the other people who were going through the door at the same time, had noticed a thing; I could tell this by Sieg's quizzical expression as he looked at me and by everyone else's unconcern. There seemed nothing else to do but stop, take a handkerchief from my purse, and dry my legs. By this time I had remembered the previous occasion on which this had happened and was more than a little puzzled about why it was happening again and what it could possibly mean.

I have spent a great deal of time wondering what these experiences mean, asking why these things keep happening, strange things like the water and the day I saw the fish in the window well outside the library window. I know it was no hallucination. I was within a yard of the window. I peered at the fish so closely because I thought it strange that it was there at all. And to add to the strangeness, I'd never seen a fish before or since that had markings like this one. I've asked people who would know about fish; I've looked in encyclopedias and I have never been able to find anything that even comes close to what I saw. But why, why? What purpose did it serve to have it there one minute, only to disappear a minute later? Had I not been home alone, I would have suspected someone of playing games.

The one time this type of phenomenon seemed to have some possible meaning was the morning I was sitting in the breakfast room just off the kitchen while I was waiting for some bread to rise. To occupy the time I was leafing through a current magazine and was sitting with my back to three windows that were hung with steel Venetian blinds. The peace and quiet of the morning were suddenly shattered by a sharp crashing sound that a steel blind would make if you landed a hard blow with a fist in the middle of it. I quickly turned in my chair to find the blind on my right jumping and swinging and banging the window frame with such violence that it took quite some time for it to come to a complete stand-still.

It was about an hour after this that Bob came home from the office and told me that the lady who had formerly owned our "haunted" bed was trying to get in touch with me. I called her back and asked what the problem was, thinking she had the wrong number or had lost it. But as it turned out, the number she had was correct and she said the phone rang repeatedly. Since I had been home all morning and had never heard the phone ring, I just assumed it was out of order, but none-the-less I was curious to know at what time she had tried to call. She told me it was ten-thirty, exactly the time that the blind was carrying on so.

Random activity by discarnate entities

There have been other times when I've been convinced that such activity as we've been discussing is just a matter of discarnate entities who happened to be around at the moment, people like you and me who want to be recognized, want you to know they're there. The problem is that we're operating in different spheres, they in the unobstructed and we in the obstructed. Evidently they don't have to wait until there is some great earth-shaking pronouncement to be made but can come to us out of companionship, love, and the desire to participate. How else can you explain such things as that which happened the evening Karl and Sieg were sitting chatting in Sieg's room, when a beautiful clear note suddenly rang out from the latter's cello, standing in the corner. Or what happened on the evening we had guests and when the conversation got around to this subject one of the guests professed disbelief in no uncertain terms. Just as she did so, a loud thump came from the drawing room ceiling. The upstairs was immediately investigated, but no one was there and nothing had fallen. I don't know whether our guest went home convinced but she went home pale. I'll never forget the day I was in the library reading and when it began to darken as the evening progressed, I looked up toward the shade and thought: "If I weren't so lazy, I'd get up and raise the shade and get at least another half hour's reading in." As I sat there thinking this I was all curled up in the chair, my feet tucked under me, chin in hand. I was loath to move. As it turned out I didn't have to, for before my startled eyes I saw the shade begin to move, gently roll itself up and quietly stop just a few inches from the top. I thought it terribly decent of them to be so accommodating.

One day an interesting letter came to us from a lady who had a similar type of experience. No great event had called forth this spirit; it was either just a friendly encounter or someone close who "cared." Here is the letter as she wrote it.

> It is nice to know that other sane and solid citizens have ghosts or poltergeists. I used to have one I suppose would fall into the poltergeist category.
>
> I lived alone and he used to rap on the closet door (I suppose he lived in there) at seven in the morning if I wasn't up and doing. I appreciated this no end, for seven was the latest I dared lie abed. Then I moved out here. Then he got rather playful and used to rap from inside the closet at odd hours during the night. I didn't mind him.
>
> When I remarried he went away, figuring, I suppose, that I no longer needed his guardianship. I'm not being facetious. This is true. I just accept the existence of poltergeists, E.S.P., etc., but have never tried to find out the why, just gratefully accept the things that have been done this way.

It happened that when all these phenomena first began, I was very active in a little theatre group. My sister, Mary, had come from St. Louis for her annual visit and at the same time to catch the current play. The evening of her arrival was "dress rehearsal." Consequently, during the afternoon she was helping me assemble my different costume changes and all the many accessories that went with each change. As each item was taken care of it was checked off a long list; when we got to the item "rings" I went to get a special make-up kit in which I always kept my theatrical make-up as well as a set of rings used only for plays. They consisted of a wedding band and engagement ring with artificial diamonds.

When I got the make-up kit out of storage and opened it up all the usual things were there, including the engagement ring, but no wedding band. After a long and fruitless search in all the special places, we looked through all my other costume jewelry, drawers, old purses, all to no avail.

When we arrived at the theatre that evening I went directly to my dressing room and immediately began the preparations for the evening's performance. As I opened my make-up kit I was astounded to see both rings lying there together. In great excitement I dashed upstairs to tell my sister who was as non-plussed as I was. I wore the rings through the run of the play, taking them off every night and leaving them at the theatre along with all the other costuming.

On the last night of the play, I didn't bother to take off my costume and make-up since there is quite a lot of work involved in packing up and cleaning out the dressing room. After I had arrived home I happened to look down at my hand and was stunned to notice that only one ring was there, the engagement ring; the wedding band was gone! I knew it couldn't have fallen off since the other ring was on top of it, and it was too tight a fit anyway. I was positive I had not taken it off. There would have been no reason to do so, but to make absolutely sure I immediately went through everything that I had come in contact with at any time that evening. I never did find that ring and I have never seen it since and that has been nearly seven years ago. In looking back it would seem that "someone" brought it back for me to use just for the play.

The theatre building itself proved to be a fascinating place. I hadn't been there long before I began hearing talk of its being haunted, but having no acquaintance at all at that time with such an area of possibility, I thought it all pretty silly. However, one night while we were gathered around a big table reading a script there was a crash in the adjoining kitchen. We went out to find that a large can that had been sitting on the stove had somehow flown off and crashed across the room. In the months and years to come this continued to happen off and on; one time it might be a lid, another time a salt cellar or a variety of other things.

I remember well Bob spending a night there with the director because the night before he had been awakened out of a sound sleep by the creaking of a rocking-chair that for no apparent reason had started rocking in the middle of the night.

Another night I received a telephone call from the same director who, to judge from his tone and manner, was obviously badly shaken. He told me that he had been in the theatre all alone building a set, and was busily occupied hammering some nails into a post. At one point, just as he was striking a blow a piercing scream rent the air. He said he felt as if he'd just struck someone a terrible blow. One can well imagine that such an experience could be quite shattering.

It was our custom after a long rehearsal in the evening to lock up the theatre and go have a bite to eat before returning home. We would always leave the windows closed and the lights out. It would nearly always happen that when we returned the small windows on the third floor would be open and a light on. Of course there was always a great deal of hilarity about who was going to go up and close the windows and turn off the light. If it was the director who went up, his cat, who followed him every place, would always stop dead at the foot of the stairs and refuse to go further.

The door opening on to the stairway fit perfectly and had a very good catch. In spite of this, the door was always being found open. One night the occupants of the theatre at that time were roused by the sound of a heavy chain clanking down the staircase. When they came into the hall to investigate, the door was again standing open, although they remembered distinctly it being closed when they went to bed. There was nothing in sight that could have possibly made such a terrible noise.

A drowned child returns home

One of the most fascinating stories we heard took place here in Denver in a local orphanage. One night after lights were out, one of the little boys looked up from his dormitory cot to see something standing at the foot of his bed. In the dim light he could make out a white shirt and knickers; he could see a hair line but the face was only a blur of light. The apparition stayed there for some minutes looking down the rows of beds. When asked how he knew it was an apparition the boy said "Because it had no legs." The boy upon seeing the apparition called out, "Who is it?" This caused the other boys to look up and when questioned later about half of the forty boys in the dorm described having seen the same apparition.

The next night one of the nuns at the orphanage had the experience of hearing a knocking on the door of her room. When she called out asking who was there she received no reply. As she attempted to rise from her bed to investigate the knocking, she found herself held to her bed by an invisible force. After some bit of a struggle she managed to get to her feet; when she opened her door she found herself looking directly at a large mass of soft glowing light.

The following night the apparition appeared again to several of the residents. This time the other nuns and the priest were called. The priest told the assembled group that he felt sure it was the little boy at the orphanage who had drowned the week before, since all the children described the apparition's clothing as being the uniform of the school. The priest felt the child was lost and therefore had come back to the only place he's ever known—the orphanage. It was decided that a mass should be held for him the next morning and that all should attend and pray for him. This was done and the children's prayers for their playmate must have been very effective, for the little boy's apparition was never seen again.

Alfred N. Whitehead is noted for saying that "The mutual adaptation of the several factors in an occasion of experience, is beauty." To me this is also representative of truth. How could anyone look at the way the different factors adapt themselves in these occasions of experience and say that they do not represent a truth or truths? There are too many to be called chance, they give too much meaning to the occasion to be called coincidence and are witnessed by too many to be called hallucinatory or hysterical.

Truth is where you find it

If you are possessed of even a grain of intelligence, what choice do you have but to question and to take your answers where you find them. We are constantly appalled, as new cases come to our attention, that they took place when we were children or before we were born, and we ask in amazement, "Why did we never know of this?" "Why are just a special few exposed to these things?" How much it could have meant to us all these years; how many answers it could have provided!

Each person finds his answers at a different point. What was the one convincing point to me would probably not mean a thing to someone else. But when you do find it, you will be amazed how you can arrive, in an instant, at the solution of the mystery or existence. After decades of questioning, all I had to do was hear the yelping of a little dead dog to know without doubt that animals survive bodily death and I therefore felt it safe to assume that if animals survived so surely must humans.

We personally find it most comforting to know that our loved ones are there in the wings waiting patiently until our performance is over, and are so hoping that when we take our final bow and the curtain is rung down they will greet us with joyful Bravos! for a job well done.

My mother died when I was a very little girl and never for

one day did I cease to miss her. Every night when I went to bed I would lie there and talk to her even though I thought that she was completely lost to me. Those empty dark hours were so completely frightening, so devoid of any hope. My whole life was ruled by what I thought she might want me to do. Before any decision was made I asked myself first, "Would my mother be proud of me if I did this or that, or would it make her feel ashamed?" As the traumas of life came and heaped themselves one upon another, there were times when my desolation knew no bounds. What it would have meant to have known, then, that I was not alone!

It makes you catch your breath to think what a little enlightenment might do for all the dark ugly corners of the world. If we should just have the courage to look and ask and dare to hope, what a transformation it could bring to an apathetic world! Is there anyone who truly believes that the unexamined life is worth the living? Or that the effort of the asking might not be worth the answer? I cannot think it so, for in my years in the world I have learned many things and one of them is, that it is not only little girls who cry in the dark, but the whole of the world!

Chapter 13

Comprehensive Living

We have traveled quite a distance together since describing the floating cigarette lighter at the beginning of this book and the other unconventional physical "things" that aroused our interest and provoked our train of thought. Now, what is the practical application of what we have learned; how can it be applied to today's everyday living, to make our temporary visit on this planet earth more meaningful, more purposeful, richer with accomplishment?

Let us consider ourselves and others as essentially consisting of three inter-related parts—body, mind, and soul— and, taking into consideration the hypotheses we have proposed, let us apply them to ourselves, our problems, and our goals in a systematic way. For our numerologist friends, that seemingly inevitable number "three" raises its head again. There seem to be three large categories of application as follows:

1. Know Thyself

Body—Realize and accept your physical limitations. If you are short in stature, don't weep because you can't see over the others at a parade—work yourself to the front row! Make the best of what God gave you to work with. It isn't the quantity but the quality that matters. Through temperance and regular maintenance keep that fine mechanism you are endowed with (your body) in good condition at all times.

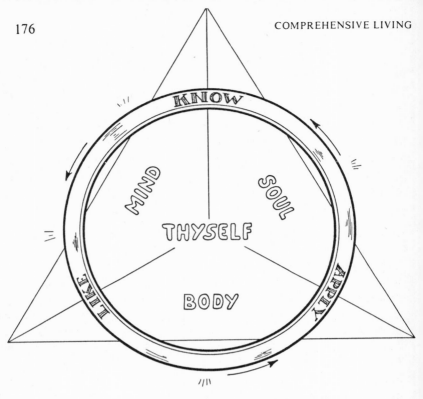

FORMAT OF COMPREHENSIVE LIVING

Figure 2

Mind—Recognize in yourself the perceptual abilities (instincts) we have illustrated and put them to work for your self-betterment. Learn to recognize and utilize so-called "intuition," which includes telepathic, clairvoyant, pre-cognitive, and astral influences.

Individuals who recognize these influences and act upon them become the dynamic leaders of our community. Tests illustrating that personal achievement, success or failure, correlates with precognition ability were described in an article, "Beyond the Senses Once Termed Fakery by Many, ESP Study Wins More Tolerance," which appeared in *The Wall Street Journal,* Wednesday, November 17, 1965. Subconscious precognition ability was measured by an IBM computer utilizing a punch card system wherein the subject strove to predict what numbers a machine would later select at random. The results showed a higher score for successful executives than for the unsuccessful, and an even lower than chance score in the phlegmatic failures.

To know thyself is of necessity a matter of total awareness. When this concept is posed to the man on the street he is more often than not likely to be very glib in his reply, readily assuring you that he knows himself quite well and is completely in charge. But ask the same man or woman for the "whys" of their likes or dislikes or for the reasons behind their idiosyncrasies; ask for an explanation of their intolerance of a particular race of people or type of personality, and chances are you will draw a complete blank.

Achieving total awareness of self

Achieving total awareness of self is a life-long project of self-discipline. It is a staunch refusal to yield to a thousand different temptations, lying to yourself which takes the form of making excuses for yourself, hiding from yourself which takes on even more devious forms. The training of a mind is from the very first a preparation for battle, for daily, almost hourly choice. Unless one is well grounded in the fundamental principles of honesty, integrity, tolerance, humility, compassion and a number of others of equal importance, his "choice" may not always be a wise one. In the making of daily and hourly choices, no one sits down and goes through such a list, checking them off one by one, but simply to be aware, to be cognizant of these principles lessens the chance of making the wrong turn, making the mistake we might forever regret.

These principles can be thought of as basic tools to be used in the mind's daily battle for progression. The next most valuable tool that can be added to the list is intuition. Intuition in itself is a gem of many hues. It encompasses all of the subliminal perceptions we have discussed aided by spirit overlay (the people in the wings) with the selective action of reason and logic.

Intuition can be thought of as a "listening," and in order to listen well one must become sensitive to an acute degree. Sensitivity can be increased and developed by listening intently to the miraculous workings of your own self and the world around you, and so the two work hand in glove. This listening to the inner self doesn't mean that you must sit and meditate for hours on end, although meditation is certainly a basic part of it. You can listen while you're walking down a busy street or stirring a cake in your own kitchen. Listen, listen carefully to the stirrings within yourself; you will hear more than the systolic and diastolic physical effects: you will hear all the kaleidoscopic interaction of events in your life that are about to become.

In my own life the mistakes I have made on important issues were due entirely to my refusal to listen to this inner self, before I knew these inner warnings could be relied upon. One of our children was having some difficulty in school, due to many years of illness. It was decided by all the professional advisors for a variety of reasons that he should be sent to a boarding school. In spite of the fact that I could not see that this would gain us a thing, I went along with this decision, since I assumed that these learned, qualified men had all the answers.

The plans and preparation went along fine, and on the appointed day we arrived at the scheduled time and promptly read all printed signs, directives and schedules and correctly followed directions and orders and deposited our weak, frightened, and sickly child in a bare and ugly room. As we turned to go to the order of more directives enforced by buzzers and bells, I tried to keep my voice steady and knees stiff long enough to say "goodbye" in a peculiar hollow voice which was supposed to represent bravado. But when I looked at his little white face and empty frightened eyes and he said, "Mama, what do I do now?" I *knew* this was no way to make a little sick boy well, nor any way to help an introverted, frightened child adjust to the world.

Had I relied then on what I intuitively knew to be right, I would have saved us all years of useless heartache, but I was too afraid of labels like—"possessive mother," "The silver cord," "Mama's boy," and so I left him there to suffer and I went home to suffer, spending the following days and months trying to learn to be strong. It took me a long time to learn that real strength is having the courage to do what you instinctively and intuitively know to be right, at least for you and yours.

Knowing thyself encompasses not only knowing how to make the wisest decisions in your everyday world but knowing what your mind is capable of in relation to your body. You read about giving your children a head start, you see on television how to fortify them with special vitamins, a special bread or cereal for a balanced diet, and of course all these things are very necessary. But nowhere do I read about how children could be fortified for life with a sound, working knowledge of all that their minds are capable of doing for them.

I am of the opinion that if children were taught from the very beginning, that there is an ever present source of help, that life is a challenge and not a picnic; that they were sent here to grow by overcoming; that there are always goals to fight for, wrongs to right; that in a very short time we should be hearing much less about the "sick society" and a great deal more about the great strides made in inner space as well as outer. While cultivating your mind helps you to lead a more interesting life, knowing how to make use of your mind helps you to lead a healthier life, as is shown in the chapter on faith healing and in our own personal experiences in learning to "know thyself."

The "open mind" possibilities

I had already been through several experiences in which the word "faith" played seemingly little if any part. For to begin with it wasn't that I had faith, it was just that I was desperate and had an "open" mind. And still it worked because, of course, the open mind allowed the effective functioning of the subconscious.

This last experience I am speaking of was many years in the making. For nearly twenty years I had an extremely painful metatarsal joint in the right foot. In that same amount of time I had been to, I can't think how many, doctors in several different cities. I went to foot doctors, internists, and bone specialists. I've worn special shoes, supports, braces, lifts, pads, and arches, all giving a very small amount of help. One day I went to see an orthopedic specialist for whom I have the greatest respect. He X-rayed my foot which showed bony spurs on the surface of the joint—a form of arthritis. He suggested surgical correction, which of course would entail, hospitalization, time in bed, a cumbersome cast, great inconvenience, and, above all, the probability of a life-long limp, which to a woman who has many duties, including running a large home and caring for children, made the thought of surgery formidable indeed.

When the human mind runs into something which it cannot cope with or cannot accept, if it is "open" it will begin to cast around for other answers, other solutions; and mine was no exception. Luckily I remembered a book I had read many years before by Rebecca Beard, M.D., called *Everyman's Search*,[1] a book I was so impressed with at the time I had added it to my own

---

[1]Rebecca Beard, M.D., *Everyman's Search* (New York: Harper & Row, Publishers, Inc., 1950).

collection. I went back and carefully re-read it, making careful mental notes. Then I began doing as she suggested, thinking as she suggested, and within one week I was walking without a limp, without special gadgets in my shoes and without pain for the first time in twenty years, I really don't know why it took me so long to come to this way of helping my foot, when I had already had such success with my various allergies.

This summer our children had a house guest from another state. He had been here only a very short while when he began to have severe problems with hayfever. He asked for an antihistamine pill and became extremely upset when he was informed that although this was a doctor's house, we never kept any. When he insisted that it was most necessary that he have some, the other boys looked at him with a tolerant and unconcerned attitude and said, "Oh, don't be silly. Just lie down and think it away," and proceeded to ignore the problem. The next morning when he came down for breakfast he reported that he felt much better and said "Now that I've conquered ragweed and dust, I'll have to start working on the foods I'm allergic to."

To know thyself well, one must spend a certain amount of time in introspection. This is not being selfish or self-centered. If you don't know who you are, how can you know what you aspire to? Or how can you be a better person tomorrow if you have no idea who or what you are today?

Knowing yourself involves a realization that your present is an amalgamation of all your pasts. In most instances past experiences in this life are beneficial and serve to strengthen "you" and make you a more wholesome and well adjusted individual. Some of us have had difficult obstacles placed in our paths that were meant, through conquest, to bring about further development. Perhaps in exploring your past you encounter experiences that are not *directly* beneficial. Perhaps your father did not create an image that you would want to mold yourself after. Instead of being a strong knight in shining armor astride a pure white steed, your father-image may better fit that of a spineless weakling. Does this mean you must necessarily go skulking through life as an animal with your "tail between your legs" feeling sorry for yourself? It does not! You can make lemonade out of your lemons from the past. You can become an even better parent than you would have been—by creating a deliberate contrast to the pitiful example that was held before you—and make such experiences *indirectly* beneficial.

Bury the garbage of past mistakes

Do not whine an excuse to someone that, "I am weak because I had such a terrible childhood." That strong person you are addressing could very well have had an even worse one than yours. Bury the garbage of past mistakes—yours and of those around you. Be selective in your memories and put only the roses of beautiful past experiences in your book of memoirs, not the sacks of garbage!

Above all, keep that mind of yours *open*. Know thyself via the clear view thus obtained. By recognizing the sources of your prejudices, fears, and apparent inadequacies, you can resolve them. There is nothing so refreshing as the breeze through an open mind.

Soul—To fully know thyself we have learned that experiences in this particular earth life are not the whole story. The current sub-conscious mind also serves as a window through which we obtain an occasional glimpse of our soul, our total personal agent, and its relationship to the Supreme Being.

There is a game we play: a question is asked, and you can list three answers in order of their importance to you. The question is—Who are you? Some will say (1) "I am Mary Jones, (2) I am a teacher, (3) I am a housewife." Others will say (1) "I am a musician, (2) I am a mother, (3) I am a wife." It is amazing how few will say first (1) "I am a child of God," and then list the other things that they are. I think that we do not relate easily and naturally to the concept of ourselves first and foremost as being children of God, and we do not start our prayers "Dear loving Father," partly because of the teachings of so many of our churches. They describe God as a super-demanding, tyrannical creature-like person "up there" somewhere who becomes irate over such trivia as little boys playing ball on Sunday and rant and rave about the "wrath of God," instead of dwelling on His love. If you have trouble knowing yourself in relation to this type of God, then perhaps it is because your God is too small.

How much more security we could know, how much more beautifully we could relate to our fellow man and the total universe if we could get away from thinking of God as a peevish, vindictive God and think of him rather as being unlimited by any of our little sects or creeds, unlimited in his ability to do, to see, to be. This God is in the moonbeam, the acorn, the stream, the wind and the air that you breathe. For God is love, honor, and justice and every intangible that holdeth the heart.

But the question that keeps tugging at you is—Where do you stand in relation to all of creation. Do you think you're not noticed, that there's no one to care? Have you forgotten what is said? "Every hair on your head is counted" and "Not a sparrow falleth. ..." Who else but your God would give you such care?

If we are honestly trying to evaluate our stand, to spiritually know ourselves, the one criterion for feeling justified in our position is the ability to answer a resounding, positive, "Yes" to such questions as—Am I making the world a better place to live in? Am I contributing beauty? Am I lending a helping hand without first making sure I will be glorified for it? You can't scan a list like that very long without soon learning what sort of a person you really are.

And lastly, the most important thing of all is to love so much what you are doing and feel proud enough of who you decided to be, that success or failure in the tangible things of life is only secondary. This will at least assure you that should you have success, you won't find yourself standing there saying "Well, now that I'm here, so what?" You will know what, because all along the way you cared intensely. And your success will not be as dust in your mouth.

Life not only gives us the opportunity to learn who we are and what we are but provides different avenues of travel on our road to becoming. These roads are as multiple and varied as the sands of the sea, and each person must find his own. The way, the path in itself, is not important as long as we are headed in the right direction. Nor is it important while we are in the process of traveling, whether we say our beads, memorize passages from the Bible, recite from the Koran, read from the Torah, meditate on the Baghavida Gita, or quote from the Vedas. The thing that *is* important is that we understand that the life of the spirit transcends the human span and that this is the only true reality; and that no matter by what road we traveled, when we reach the top of the hill we join as one voice in a mighty "Gloria in Excelsis Deo."

2. Like Thyself

Body—We do not mean that you should spend endless vain hours preening yourself before a mirror and getting "choked-up" over your own image. Rather, you should cheerfully accept whatever God has granted you for a body and be proud of the possession—regardless! You need not be a Greek god or goddess in appearance. More than one comedian has taken a bad feature, turned it to his advantage and made a handsome living from it. As a doctor, I have found poor bodily posture to be primarily caused by a feeling of "not liking my body" and a resulting subconscious humping-over in a vain attempt to be inconspicuous.

Mind—There is one word I would like to strike permanently from the dictionary and also strike its dreadful meaning from human experience; it is the word "guilt." "I don't like me." "I don't think I am a very nice person." How many hundreds of times have I heard these statements in hypnotic trances induced due to nearly every variety of behavioral personality problem in the book, yet all having the same basic cause—living with someone they don't like, themselves!

There is not one among us who has not made some pretty pitiful mistakes in his or her past. If he or she who is without sin is to cast the first stone none will be thrown.

We have all "erred" in days gone by. Let us recognize this, then do an annual spring house-cleaning of our minds and briskly brush away the cobwebs of past mistakes and carefully treasure the good things. Regularly clean out and sort the contents of your mental attic. Such action is labeled "the power of positive thinking" by Dr. Norman Vincent Peale. Put aside the thoughts that are not uplifting and dwell on those that are.

This is a large order and if you can accomplish it on a conscious level yourself, more power to you. However, if you find difficulty here, ask for help and utilize an objective advisor and the sub-conscious approach via hypnotherapy. The more effective suggestibility of the altered awareness of the subconscious mind was not put there to entertain friends in nightclub acts, remember!

Replace guilt feelings with feelings of *responsibility*. Recognize your past mistakes and sincerely determine to do better in the future. The resulting good, clean feeling of knowing you are doing your best to do what is right makes you comfortable to live with. You become a nice person to know, especially to yourself.

Resolve all subconscious-conscious conflicts. *Be* the kind of person you really are. Do not be two-faced and hypocritical. "Hateful to me as are the gates of hell is he who hideith one thing in his heart—yet uttereth another" is a wise old saying of unknown origin. A bad conscience is the result of thinking or believing one way yet doing another. What an uncomfortable way to live. Such two-facedness can get you into serious trouble, for it is the beginning of the path that leads to a split personality or schizophrenia. As Shakespeare put it so well, "To thine own self be true, and it will follow as night follows day, thou cans't then be false to no one."

Hypocrisy is transmitted telepathically more rapidly and effectively than any other vice. Haven't you met people that you "instinctively" felt could not be trusted, that you knew immediately were two-faced? Such internal conflict (conscious vs. subconscious) not only results in not liking thyself but you will find eventually others sharing your dislike of you. And don't try to fool yourself that your acting ability will suffice to cover-up your inner-most thoughts. Telepathy has been around for a long time, and will be.

Wear a clean mind like you wear clean clothing. You will be more comfortable and so will those about you. And remember, you are always you, there is no escape from yourself, not even in bodily death. The personal "you" persists, always and forever.

After all, there is, as Jean-Paul Sartre expresses so vividly in his play with the same title, *No Exit.*

Soul—If the soul or spirit is master over the mind and the mind is the master of the body, then it is obvious that if we are desirous of living a life where all are in harmony, we must begin at the beginning and come to grips with our soul. The disharmony of soul, mind and body often resulting from guilt feelings, gives rise to most of our problems and illnesses. Only by resolving this disharmony is it really possible to like thyself, and this self-like is the first prerequisite for leading a well-balanced and productive life.

The Catholic Church recognizes the need of the disturbed individual to verbalize his conflicts and very wisely provided the confessional. For some people the most difficult thing in the world is to say "I made a mistake and I'm sorry," and follow it with "What can I do to make amends," but this very process is the most basic of all. The one common denominator all men have can be summed up in one word, *imperfection.* Making mistakes is common to all. The sin comes in not caring or not trying to rectify them.

Speak your mind courageously

Nothing will assure you of greater success in your efforts to like yourself than having the honesty and courage to speak your mind, especially if it is an unpopular thought or for an unpopular cause or belief. It has long been said that, if all men accept without question the truth presented to them, then that phase of truth needs changing and some stronger form is required. If you have first studied your cause or beliefs carefully, become convinced of the goodness or the justice or the truth of them, have the courage to take your stand even to the point where you are careless of defeat, then your success in liking yourself is guaranteed. Diogenes taught that no man could be a slave except to his own intemperances, and I think that applies even more so to his own fears and cowardices.

From the very practical standpoint it is so much cheaper to be good than to pay the price of being bad; from any and all points of view, whether it be paying with a nagging guilty conscience, and the sometimes resulting illness of either body or mind, or the even more mundane problem of feeling the necessity to buy a stained-glass window for the church in your efforts to salve your conscience or pave the way ahead. Nothing nullifies the possibility of future misery like present virtue.

3. Apply Thyself

Body—If you are presented with that beautiful car and do not use it but let it sit idly in the garage, no matter how fine a mechanism you started out with, corrosion will gradually, then rapidly, deteriorate it until it will no longer function. The same holds for the human body. It was made to be used. In contrast to the early pioneer days when those who didn't physically work didn't eat, today we tend to be button pushers and spectators.

My patients are routinely urged to get regular exercise, at least once a week involving such vigor that deep breathing is required to the point of *physical* exhaustion. They may complain that they are already tired at the end of each day—why should they make themselves more tired? But, this is nervous exhaustion, and what we are talking about is true physical exhaustion. The stronger the heart beats, the faster the blood flows through the "pipes," the less corrosion can accumulate. But it must be calm, regular exercise, not frantic, spasmodic, and only occasional. At Bradmar we have five hungry fireplaces and the proverbial woodpile which serves as an assignment for the "hungry bums" of our family. Work first, eat second. For more urban dwellers may we suggest—walking up the stairs instead of using the elevator, walking to work instead of riding, doing so many lengths in the swimming pool that deep breathing expands the lowermost air-pockets of the lungs, doing that yard work and construction *yourself,* and of course—golf, tennis, skiing, bike-riding, etc.

As a past-president of a men's service club, I highly approve organized activities that benefit others, as well as self. They make you feel not only physically but morally better

Mind—We have repeated before and shall here again: the human mind, like the body, was put there to be used! It is a very real function, not a phantasy. Use it. Not only to know and like yourself but in relationship to others as well. There are very few hermits in modern times. We are a gregarious society and as such must learn to live in harmony with each other. The rapidity of transportation has figuratively shrunk the planet earth until we are literally one society. The goal of peace on earth can best be obtained when we project thoughts of trust and affection not only between individuals but between groups and nations.

Apply the many listed functions of the subconscious towards this goal. Remember, experiments in E.S.P. have yet to show any limitations of powers or functions imposed because of distance. Clean your mental back yard of old prejudices against others of different color, customs, or culture. We are all made in God's image.

Soul—There are very few things that upset my (D.B.B.) Piscean nature to the point of becoming truly angry, and the one thing that does it without fail is to hear someone say "I don't want to become involved." To keep from becoming involved is not to live, for this is what life and living is all about. Only by becoming involved can you apply the soul's learning, the results of all the ages of experiencing, struggling and progressing; the end result of the knowing and the liking. Our whole reason for being here is to learn and to grow as a natural consequence of the experiences caused by the constant interaction of the different phases of existence: ourselves in relationship to our siblings, our peers, our environment and our government.

Those who are too afraid of life to become involved usually steel themselves to observing life pass by without having any reaction or emotion about it. They like to think they are being sophisticated, but such aloofness is hardening and will lead to unhealthy mental habits and eventually to a life of constant evasion from facing reality.

It takes a certain amount of maturity to choose wisely and to know when and how much to become involved and where to stop short, to know beyond what point caring becomes meddling or invasion. But know that *there is that point* and if you're in charge of yourself, you will be honest about where the line is. Beyond that you leave the other person free even to do what is bad for him.

There is no phase of one's existence that cannot be benefited by these preceding steps, whatever your role in life may be, parent, teacher, or counselor. Most of life's roles place us in the position of counseling, officially or unofficially, somewhere, sometime, and to setting an example for someone else. It would be well for all of us to remember the familiar saying "What you do speaks so loudly I can't hear what you say."

I remember a very funny story told to us by a friend about a mutual acquaintance. It was at the time the said acquaintance was teaching a Sunday-School class. She was by nature a very dynamic, straightforward sort of woman and could at times be rather short-tempered. On one particular Sunday morning when the children were being unusually unruly, noisy and unmanageable, she, being pushed to the point of near hysteria, finally screamed "Sit down and be quiet, God dammit, while I tell you about Jesus!"

I feel this an excellent story to keep in mind, for children nearly always tend to do as you do, rather than do as you say. Nothing is as effective in teaching as setting an example rather than forcing others into stringent patterns of behavior. The very act of setting an example necessitates applying your knowledge, to apply your knowledge necessitates becoming involved. To live is to become involved, to become involved is to care, and to care is the essence of being.

Like all practicing physicians I was primarily trained to treat physical disorders. Precious little time was spent in medical school training on how to treat disorders of the mind and soul. These problems were delegated to the specialty—trained psychiatrists, and because these doctors were primarily oriented toward Freud (God is a neurotically projected father image!) any treatment regarding the soul or spiritual values was left up to the local parish priest or minister. He, in turn, may be very spiritually oriented but has had no real training in the psychology of the mind and may be unknowingly compounding the problem by adding or enforcing guilt feelings.

This piecemeal approach to dealing with human problems was and is pitifully inadequate judging by the poor results. People don't go about in separate pieces.

Upon entering practice, I found to my bewilderment that about eighty percent of the problems of my patients were emotional or spiritual and of those few that were obviously physical the emotional or spiritual overlay was more important than the physical component. I dutifully repaired the physical defects then sent the ones with major emotional problems to the psychiatrists and the ones with major spiritual problems to their religious leaders. However, it didn't seem to work. They kept coming back through the same door through which they left—unchanged, unhelped, as bothered and bewildered as before. The piecemeal approach seemed to be most ineffective.

The reading, study, and observations provoked by the occurrences of the paranormal physical phenomena, as described, resulted in the gradual development of an awareness of fellow humans as whole beings. The complicated inter-relationships of body-mind-soul become increasingly more evident then in every human situation that I encountered, be it pregnancy, frigidity, infertility, menstrual disorders, depression, anxiety, menopause, etc. Accordingly, from the depths of my subconscious came the double-labeled triangle described and illustrated and assigned me "by George" to use as an outline to follow in treating my patients, not as mechanical robots, not as mere baby factories (past, present, or future) but comprehensively as total beings. Now, "by George," it works! Applying this format as a guide to follow, I found the patients becoming better adjusted. I've had bone-crushing grips from beaming husbands, "She's a different woman now!" Now I don't mean to imply that this format is an all-encompassing myth that will solve all problems of all people. There is a long, hard road to traverse between recognizing and resolving conflicts. In teaching young doctors and medical students, I repeatedly stress, "You can't cure them all! Don't expect to."

This was quoted back to me by my reassuring and understanding wife the other day when I came home defeated and muttering in exasperation. I had spent many hours patiently holding a mental and spiritual mirror up before a patient and had erroneously thought I was making headway. She was involved in her fourth divorce proceeding in just a few short years, blaming each marriage failure on the other person, of course. The lady was quite attractive physically and a natural blond. She was very vain about her lovely hair and proud that it was not artificially produced as most is today. After the third hypnosis session in which I strove to get her attention off her body and to get *her* to see what I saw in her mind and soul, I was feeling quite sure that progress was being made until my ego was shattered by her parting statement; that had me muttering in frustration as I arrived home. She had stated that if God would just grant her one wish, one little favor, then she would have no other problems and her husbands would not leave her. Expecting some deep and profound mental or spiritual insight to be forthcoming as a consequence of my careful guidance, I was not prepared for—"If God would just grant me natural dark eyebrows to go with my blond hair, then I wouldn't have such a blank look when I first awaken in the morning. I don't want anyone to see me before I use eyebrow pencils."

No, you can't cure them all, but using the format we have developed as a guide for comprehensive living, let's hold it over a few major problems that beset modern mankind and see if, perhaps, we can help solve them. I have been doing this for years now and sincerely believe that although it failed to darken this one lady's eyebrows, it serves as a more efficient guide to self-awareness and self-adjustment to stress, judging again by results, than any other approach I have used or observed others using. To help you carefully apply it to your life, let's cite some examples and demonstrate its application.

Marriage counseling

In the United States nearly fifty percent of the marriages end up on the rocks—annulment, desertion, divorce. Our educational system seems to teach typing, tap-dancing, and tom-foolery but not preparation for parenthood, not how to live with each other. It is true that the circumstances in some marriages may justify their being dissolved, but these are few and far between. The basic structure of any civilized community or culture is still and always will be marriage and the home. Let's apply our format where applicable to the problems that arise when a man and woman decide to live with each other, "until death do us part."

Superimposing our triangle, let's consider the "know thyself" first. A marital union should be properly joined in body, mind, and soul (the inner triangle). This is probably the reverse order of importance but let's consider the union of bodies. I would rather use the term "love" than the usual "sex" term for this union. If there is naught but physical union then sex would apply, but that occurs in the house of prostitution not in the house of holy matrimony.

The man, being the aggressor, should be well versed on the wonderful physical art of love making—is he? Where did he learn it? From his father? He couldn't. No one taught his father. From his schooling? Now, really! As a women's specialist in treating problems of frigidity, I soon learned the near-truth of the old French saying, "There is no such thing as a frigid woman, only awkward men." As a consequence we have instituted men-only classes as part of our parent training and dubbed them "Rooster-Parties." This label reflects the physical—hormone affected—necessity for the male to "crow." This male-ego phenomenon is a physical property of the male body and occurs in all species of animals, the human included. As the aggressor the male should be well versed in the physical techniques of adequate love-making. All men on earth as a consequence of their male hormones, tend to feel they are the world's greatest lovers. As a women's specialist I get an entirely different opinion from their wives. I also get an entirely different impression as I watch the unknowing wonderment in their facial expressions when I lecture on the details of the physical erotic zones of a woman and how to properly stimulate her.

Assuming acquired knowledge of the physical or bodily aspect of marital union, let's go on to the next corner of the inner triangle of our format—"mind." A proper union of minds entails having enough interests in common to establish a true companionship on a social level. A marriage based upon mere physical or body attraction will be short-lived. Many couples who were good companions prior to their weddings, or prior to their children—who went places and did things together regularly—tend to drop these shared events and settle dully into a rut of marital monotony afterward. Don't do this! Be even more mentally alert and more involved in mutual interests after marriage and after babies than you were before.[2] Realize, too, that the act of love-making is primarily a physical phenomenon to a man but is, conversely, primarily a psychological phenomenon to a woman. Sex is said, appropriately, to be located from the waist down in a man and from the neck up in a woman. You both ought to know this. Should a wife feel subconsciously resentful or hostile toward her husband, due to a variety of real or imagined irritations, he may be the world's greatest physical manipulator yet will get a cold lack of response. Bring those subconscious irritations to the surface openly and honestly, both of you. Verbalize any irritation and resolve the conflict. Do not hide one thing in your heart yet utter another. What a stupid way to live together!

Telepathy will pick up such hidden hostility and make you both miserable in each other's company. On the positive side, a man and wife who have explored each other's mind as well as body, who "know" each other in the fullest sense will feel the most comfortable when together and the most uncomfortable when apart. They would never think of hiding thoughts from each other, but freely express themselves to each other as if they were one blended mind. Frequently these happy couples "read" each other's mind telepathically regularly. Remember the wife 'at the church lecture who demonstrated telepathy by mentally asking her traveling husband in a distant state to phone her? His watch was five minutes late, but he read her mind immediately, as usual, for they really "know" each other mentally.

A doctor friend in a club I spoke to described to me afterward how he had been in the armed forces during the war and while stationed in France was awakened from sleep with the realization his wife had had their baby. Correcting for distance factors, the time he awakened correlated exactly with the time of birth. Hundreds of examples of E.S.P. come from proper emotional and mental union of married minds who know each other so well. Sexual responsiveness, or rejection, in a woman is very closely related to the associated previous events of her life. Difficulty in compatibility in this sphere is very complicated and should be treated by age-regression under hypnosis by a competent counselor. Subconscious association of a poor father-image, an unadmirable father with an unsuspecting but admirable husband is

---

[2] Robert A. Bradley, M.D., *Husband-Coached Childbirth*, (New York: Harper & Row, 1965).

frequently the root of the problem. One can't be, exclusively, a women's specialist. If you two don't really know each other, ask for help.

"Until death do us part"

Knowing the remaining inner corner of our triangle, the soul, is also very important in the "until death do us part" relationship between two people. If there is a wide variation in belief between the two on where they are going and what will happen to them after death, this can become such an obstacle in their union that it affects other aspects. I recall the case of one wife I was asked to treat for a frigidity problem in which her cold unresponsiveness was based entirely on the fact her husband was an atheist and she was a devout Christian. She participated in regular church activities as did her children. She subconsciously felt she was not spiritually married, that the sacramental nature of the wedding vows were blasphemous in relation to her husband. She felt that if she wasn't spiritually united, she couldn't be fully physically or mentally united. Many mixed marriages (religious) do apparently succeed but a remarkable number do not. And the ones that seemingly succeed on the surface sometimes are under stress and stubbornly are determined to prove they can, but there cannot be the true, deep, meaningful relationship between these people here as there is between two who not only are united in *this* world but know they will continue to be united in the next.

And what a bewildering choice is imposed on the children of mixed marriages. "But we never discuss our differences before the children." Remember the telepathy experiment between mother and child, the identical brain-wave pattern of serene and disturbed dreams? You don't have to discuss it, they know, they know your differences. You can't kid kids.

If humanly possible, if spiritually possible, become one in your beliefs. It doesn't matter which denomination, it doesn't matter which creed, it matters that you both think and study in depth so that your beliefs are not idly arrived at; it matters that you set aside in your home life regular times for uplifting and inspiring thoughts; it matters that your beliefs are shared and sincere; it matters that they are so well arrived at that they penetrate to the depths of your souls and are not merely the superficial mouthings of others. Know what is, not what someone else told you ought to be. Hypocrisy is instinctively perceived and obvious to your children—and is very disturbing.

In further relation to your body, realizing your limitations, don't try to exceed them and be big enough not to resent them. People of small stature tend to be defensive or have compensating "banty-rooster" overly-aggressive personalities. They also nearly bend over backwards in a vain attempt to be taller. People of large stature tend to be apologetic and tend to hump over to become more like others. Accept and like thyself—physically; accept your body the way it is. It is not the quantity that counts, it's the quality.

Similarly, recognize the physical limitations of your spouse and accept, yea, like and praise him or her! You can't trade in your own body each year for a shiny new one; take into stride the necessary changes of age, and look upon those wrinkles and creases as "service stripes" of maturity. The same attitude should be directed towards your wife's body, gentlemen. The Hollywood habit of some paunchy, balding, egotistical male trading in his maturing forty-year-old wife on two (or more) successive twenty-year-olds is as stupid as it is repulsive. This practice of serial polygamy has gained nothing but more and more divorces, suicides, mixed-up children, and a steadily enlarging market for sleeping pills. Accept the physical manifestations of aging and maturity in your own body and in that of your life-mate. Don't frantically dye those grey hairs or copy the clothes fads of the younger generation. Don't envy the youth their physical beauty—let them have it for they have nothing else! They don't have good judgment, serenity of mind, wisdom of soul, temperance of emotions—and you do! Or you certainly should by now. Their physical beauty is temporary and declines with time; your attributes are permanent and, like good wine, become better with age.

Don't clam up—talk it out

In liking each other while living with each other, it is essential that you be honest and open about your preferences regarding techniques of love making. I cannot over-emphasize, *verbalize!* Talk to each other about likes or dislikes. How many exasperating times have I had separate sessions with a couple to find one resenting and thinking negative "dirty" ideas about his or her partner, and the other feeling this same act of intimacy to be of the highest order and an ennobling physical manifestation of spiritual love—*yet neither have ever expressed their feelings to the other!* "Nice people don't talk about such things." They do now. Intimate problems are discussed in detail in series articles in popular magazines. There is a campaign now to be rid of old laws and institute new "mutual consent" laws for all adults. Talking about, instead of hiding and resenting can save a marriage.

Why wait for the divorce court label of incompatibility when a beautiful compromise and a mutual understanding could have been achieved by simple, open, honest talk. In many instances the puritanical background of one partner (all sex is dirty!) must and can be blended with a modern background (sex is the physical expression of spiritual love) of the other.

Do not hide dislikes, bring them out in the open. Work out compromises that will result in each liking the other's mind. Again, if you need objective help here, ask for it.

No matter how well united a couple may be—body, mind, and soul—do not lose sight of the concept of individuality. The total personal agent like a snowflake is never a duplicate of another and each has the fundamental right of individuality. The underlying experiences of all former lives will inevitably manifest through the current subconscious as a particular personality that cannot be duplicated. Take joy in this. Wouldn't it be boring if we were all alike? Let your spouses have lives of their own over and above that portion devoted to being a wife or husband. Mutual trust and understanding does not imply duplication.

Weight control

Another problem becoming most common in our land of plenty is overeating. Let's superimpose the format of comprehensive living and see how it applies here.

In knowing your body, you must take into account hereditary physical factors. Some lucky people can eat all they wish of any type of food and not gain excessive weight, and the same was true of their parents. However, there is a great majority of unlucky people like ourselves who inherit just the opposite tendency. You can't change your parents so if you are in the latter category, you must change your habits. As with most worthwhile things, this isn't easy.

In addition to hereditary factors, there are other physical

factors that should be checked out by your doctor—glandular (thyroid), hormonal, etc.—as part of your routine physical care. The next corner of our triangle is the mind, and there are multiple mental and emotional overlays to the eating problem. Cultural customs set us up erroneously from earliest infancy. Whenever a baby cries the first thing the parent does is put a nipple in his mouth to partake of food. The baby may have been crying not out of hunger but out of boredom, physical discomfort, temper, hostility, etc. A conditioned reflex is thereby established in the subconscious of all of us that the treatment of stress, regardless of variety, is to eat.

This reflex established in the open, suggestible minds of human infants will be carried throughout life to manifest itself under stressful situations for ever after. This is reflected in the assuaging of grief, especially in rural areas, where the family of the loved one is showered with gifts of food from the friends and neighbors. The best and most eating I have ever done was associated with rural funerals. It is also reflected on a long-term basis by those who feel insecure, who are not comfortable in the independent state of adulthood and manifest their desire to return to dependency by subconscious compulsions to overeat. Could the overemphasis on the human breast be related to this?

In the same manner, any deprivation of food in infancy or childhood will so impress the subconscious that there will be a conscious preoccupation with food in later life. Those who have suffered from hunger in childhood are noted for becoming overweight in adulthood. It is a subconscious fortification, a laying up of stores of reserves for fear of another episode of hunger. Children of the wealthy are usually not very interested in eating. Children of the poor are overly interested and place eating as primary.

Obesity can also be a symbol of material success. The fat and sassy compared to the lean and hungry. Those who have, compared with those who have-not. A tendency reflecting the over-importance of material things compared with the thin aesthete who denies them.

Food is also established as a conditioned reward and as a symbol of victory. Do your job first and we will have a feast. We could go on and on showing the emotional and mental overlay associated with eating. The main idea here is "know thyself." Using conscious reason, recognize into which pattern you fit and by recognition resolve to bring such reflexes under control. It isn't

easy to do but it beats taking appetite suppressing "goof ball" pills
which help only temporarily and in the long run can do you harm.

Soul and eating

Now we come to the last corner of the triangle, the soul.
What involvement does the soul have with eating? Many religions
put much stress on total or partial abstinence from food, or types
of food, especially on certain special days. I think a subconscious
fear of death, like other fears at this level, can result in compen-
satory overeating—the concept of the Feast of the Last Supper,
the overfeeding of a criminal that precedes capital punishment,
etc. The religious esthetic, convinced of the rewards of the next life
disdains the importance of food in this life. The religiously guilty
or the subconsciously unconvinced tend to obssessively stuff themselves.

Severe deprivation of food in a previous life can carry over
into this one, with a subconscious building up of reserves as a
consequence. I wish we could all have accurate "life-readings" to
bring into conscious levels such carry-overs, but perhaps this was
not meant to be.

Now in considering "like thyself" applied to body, mind, and
soul, it is necessary to bring about corrective measures for any
defective mechanism brought to light by "knowing thyself."

Deliberate or compulsive overeating may be a conscious
manifestation of subconscious resentment toward a parent or other
authoritarian figure. I recall one patient, greatly overweight, who
had tried many diets, routines of pills, etc., all to no avail. Under
age-regression in hypnosis she bitterly recounted how as a teenager
she had fallen madly in love with a certain boy of whom her
mother did not approve. She had deliberately gotten pregnant by
the lad in a maneuver to force her mother to accept her marrying
him. It didn't work. Her mother marched her off to an abortionist
and ordered the boy from her life. She later reluctantly married
the boy of her mother's choice whom she gradually came to
subconsciously resent as much as her mother. It was noted that
her overeating had begun shortly after the abortion.

Her mother wanted her to be svelte and slim, and mother
became very upset when her daughter gained too much weight.
Boy did she show her!—About 200 lbs. worth of subconscious
resentment. None of this obvious mechanism was on the conscious

level until after hypnosis. Then it took a lot of hypno-suggestion to undo the harm and get this patient to like herself and quit hating her mother.

You should take personal pride in your body and its appearance and in your mind and its function. Clean house, get rid of the cobwebs. In "apply thyself" application, perform regular exercise in relation to body; use your good conscious reason to rid your subconscious of childish resentment or vindictiveness; you are made to reflect the God element and the weakness of self-indulgence does not glorify Him. I remember years ago the actor Gregory Peck playing the role of a new parish priest who when asked by a gushy corpulent woman how she could enhance her chances to enter heaven, snapped back at her, "Eat less! The gates of Paradise are narrow!"

Heart attacks

Probably the greatest shortener of life on this earth plane is the tendency to heart attacks. And if by foolish intemperance you must leave before your job is done, you have to keep coming back until you learn your lesson. There are no short-cuts on the road of life. Let's utilize our format and see, again, how it can apply here.

If in knowing yourself you find a hereditary tendency in your family, don't hit the panic button. Remember, we all must die sometime and if we had a choice, this is a nice, short, and efficient way to cross over into the unobstructed universe. In the interest of postponing this inevitable trip until you have had a long, useful, productive and enjoyable earth life, it will behoove you to behave yourself in certain fundamental ways. From the physical or body standpoint, keep your weight under control. Observe the advice just given in the previous example. Next, get regular exercise to the point of physical exhaustion once a week or oftener if feasible and, of course, get regular physical exams from your doctor. These general health measures have been stressed before; it's just that they are even more important if there is a history of heart attacks in your family.

In knowing thyself mentally, it becomes also very important that you achieve harmonization of your subconscious and your conscious mind. Trying to be two people instead of just one puts an extra strain on your heart as well as your mind. The hypocrite who lives in constant fear that his true inner self will show instead of the false self he has contrived to present to the public, is much more prone to heart attacks than the serene individual who has no such division, and no such fear.

Through careful meditative self-analysis, or via requested help, if indicated, in the form of psychoanalysis—"like thyself." Having recognized the cobwebs of petty childish carry-overs that tend to make you insecure, panicky—clean house, get rid of them. Bury the garbage of disturbing past mistakes or unfortunate associations. We all have them but we don't all drag them along with us: learn how to leave them in the past where they occurred and where they belong. Don't be a "Dodo Bird" who looks back constantly at where he's been instead of looking forward to where he's going. Substitute the clean, good feeling of responsibility for the cardiac-spasm-producing and degrading feeling of guilt. Make amends for any hurt you have done others—"Have a heart" —and a double meaning is intended.

Know thyself with regards to your soul. Make your peace with your Maker. A factor in untimely heart attacks is also a morbid fear of death. If you are in attunement and through careful study and meditation have arrived at your inner religious convictions with self-honesty, then your true attitude will be "Thy will be done." When your assigned work on the earth plane is completed, and the decision is not yours to make, you will cheerfully accept the inevitable and will not live in constant fear of not living.

In applying yourself to ward off premature heart attacks, it has been said that you should manage to control at least two out of three factors. If you can manage all three, great, but if circumstances interfere, pick any two of the three and manage them. The three factors are: (1) weight, (2) exercise, and (3) serenity.

If your work is inescapably nerve-wracking, be sure your weight is normal and see to it that regular exercise is performed. If inheritance makes proper weight a near impossibility, combine regular exercise with a form of life work and of home environment that produces serenity. If regular exercise seems impossible, keep your weight in bounds and if you don't like your work, you'd better change to what you do find soul satisfying.

The challenge for youth

Our last example of the application of the format for comprehensive living will be directed towards youth, for herein lies the hope of the world.

We were shocked into the realization of the need for this by the recent visit of a neighbor boy. On previous visits we adults had all been so impressed by this teenager's extensive vocabulary, his glib and clever tongue, his charming manners and consideration for others, his willingness to pitch in and work when our boys were involved in chores so necessary at big Bradmar. We had, as adults, often remarked on what a marvelous future Bill had before him and, as adults are prone to do, we had admiringly projected his ultimate outcome as a fine statesman, outstanding attorney, etc.

On this particular visit one of us asked him what his career plans were now that he was finishing high school. We were all horrified by the way he answered. The bright-faced sparkle of youth changed to an anxious, depressed look. He hung his head and fidgeted, looking at the floor, and stated hesitantly, "Well, I guess I'll go into the armed forces; that is the only place I can see security and a guarantee of a retirement; they take care of all your needs."

We couldn't get over the sudden change in him that our simple question had provoked. From a sparkling effervescent youth, noted for enjoying the thrill of taking chances on the ski run, on the ball field, to an anxious Casper Milquetoast, an old man afraid of taking chances, seeking security and retirement before he had even started. His sparkle changed to dull listlessness as he contemplated his future. In all reverence we thought, Good God, in this wonderful world of opportunity he is so uninspired, lacks so much self-confidence that he wants to quit before he starts!

Now the adults who were present will all admit to a firm prejudice against peacetime armed forces. I (R.A.B.) have served my time in two wars and know the necessity of armed forces in time of war. I also know how dulling such routine and discipline can be to the spirit of youth in time of peace. Not super-conformity but the daring of intelligent non-conformity is what made this nation great. This destruction of initiative by guaranteeing clothing, food, shelter and medical care is referred to disdainfully as suckling at the breast of the great eternal mother and represents, in time of peace, a sheltering haven for the mediocre who cannot meet the challenge of independence and competition.

We were shocked that he did not feel capable of developing

himself first as an individual, then offering his service to defend his country against attack, as a reservist, later, if necessary, as we had done.

Let's, as an example, superimpose the format of comprehensive living onto Bill's problem; no, not just Bill's problem but that of all youths who stand on the threshold of life and a career.

Youths as a rule know themselves physically, in relation to their young bodies, quite well. However, in relation to their minds and souls they do not see the value, yet, of such knowledge. This will eventually come with time, or it had better, for there would be nothing more foolish-looking than an elderly beatnik.

The ultimate value of knowing yourself is first for your own soul's progression and secondly for passing on to your children all you have been able to learn from your own travels in the world of experiences, without any intention of robbing them in any way of having their own. For many of the things that happen to us are not only of Karmic origin, but take place because we need the experience of having, being, doing and becoming involved.

Our young people of today are sometimes severely criticized because they become too involved and make a tremendous amount of noise and create a great deal of havoc in the process. This is usually due to the excess energy of youth and their lack of wisdom in choosing what issues are truly important and what are not. Parents and teachers could do a great service if they would prepare young people to know that in a matter of years they will change their attitudes and ideas about many things, but if they are wisely taught their basic principles will not change.

Sometimes in trying to find our own true identities, we protest too much; we want to knock down standards just because they're there. Maintaining individualism for its own sake is empty, even dangerous and ugly as in the case of the long haired, black jacketed ones who make life miserable for the many by roaring around on their motorcycles, leaving chaos and confusion in their wake. When we start having the accusing finger pointed at us as non-conformists, we would do well to stop, reconsider our individualism and ask ourselves several pertinent questions. Are we kicking over idols just because our family worshiped them? Or are we dancing like monkeys just because mother waltzed so beautifully? If the answers to these questions are all "Yes," then we had better stop for a long look and a reevaluation of ourselves.

Who and what are the thrill seekers, the doers of unmotivated crimes, the takers of drugs? Are they our young people seeking release from boredom in the thrill of crime? Could this be a rebellion against a life devoid of deeper meaning? Must we always depend on the challenge of war to bring out the bravery, self-sacrifice and initiative in our youth? I for one refuse to believe this.

Our responsibility as adults

We, the adults, have the responsibility to point out the challenges, making clear the purpose and meaning of life. But don't expect to do it by lecturing and haranguing, for it is the pattern of youth to do just the opposite when this technique is used. Youth will very seldom come right out and ask for leadership and guidance and he resents it when it is forced onto him. We must instead remember our own struggling years, how we were too proud to admit to our fears. It has always been the habit of youth to cover up their insecurity by bravado, braggery and noise. It is up to us to see through this, to recognize the symptomatic call for help.

By our own example, by the lives we lead, by the principles we stand for, by the challenges we accept, by the enthusiasm we manifest towards these challenges, by our very attitudes we must say, "No challenge today? Dear heavens child, don't just stand there. The woods are burning!" It is by the very nature of youth that once the challenge is made they very seldom run from it, for they have the spirit, the undimmed imagination, and the energy to carry it off.

Some people by the very nature of their personalities, like the Sagitarrians, will be great achievers for no other reason than to be the winner of the race, to be on top of the heap and the first in line. But for the rest of us and yes, even the Sagitarrian, it is so much more rewarding, even necessary to have a reason, a motivating power, for it is this that generates the vital energies needed for the long race. Youth must be shown and convinced that to achieve mere security, mere tangible assets are as nothing; that any victory is hollow unless accompanied by our inner growth. He must be taught that he alone in contrast to all of the rest of creation, can choose not to be insignificant.

Contemplation of death

Our trip is nearly completed. Our train of thought that began

with the floating cigarette lighter is pulling into its last station—the station of death, bodily death, for you have seen
evidences along the way that there is no other kind.

This depot, representing the last stop on the earthly trip, is
not located in a desolate desert of nothingness as tradition may
have you believe. It is more like the depot serving as an entrance
to a great, shining new metropolis where visitors are joyously
welcomed to meet with dear friends again, friends they have
missed so much, so long.

What basically have we been saying in this book if not that
there is a life after death? Not that *we* say it but that we point out
evidences here and there. What else can it mean? If our conclusions have been wrong, then who *does* "Walk at Bradmar?" Give
us a better answer, show us where we err. "This substance of
things hoped for, evidences of things not seen..."[3] What else
could it possibly add up to, these things that cannot be explained
by our present day scientific knowledge? Thomas Huxley wrote,
"Sit down before fact as a little child, be prepared to give up every
preconceived notion...."[4] I could quote to you endlessly all the
great minds who have done just this, but it would only take one
short sentence to give you the essence of their conclusions: I have
come to believe without any doubt there is no death.

How strange it seems that the golden door to the larger phase
of existence has been draped in black and labeled "DEATH" and
that it has come to be so exquisitely feared! The pain and agony
associated with what we think of as death is strictly on this side of
existence. The process of death itself is a lovely, soft experience of
dreamily fading away. Only a week ago we lost our little grandpapa; for days he continued to slip in and out of comas. When he
would return he would be asked where he had been. He would
indicate a pleasant experience and announce that—"I must take a
plane to where I am." Only when he was more fully with us would
he begin to suffer. When he slipped over we rejoiced for him that
he had completed his transition so effortlessly.

By all rights we should cry at the birth of the individual and
not at his death, for in most cases the birth signifies the beginning
of many long years of trials, tribulations and sometimes painful
learning. Inversely, we should rejoice at what we call death for it is

³ Hebrews X: 13.
⁴ Thomas Huxley in M. Lincoln Schuster, *A Treasury of the World's Great Letters,*
(New York: Simon & Schuster, Inc., 1940) p. 343.

a release from our struggles, the beginning of freedom, joy, rapturous beauty both as to sight and sound and an ever upward going on, provided of course we have earned these things. Vulnerable as we humans are to the emotions we are subjected to, we may never be able to achieve this, for we eagerly look forward to the new members of our family, and even though we feel those who depart in body from this plane are going to a better place, we cannot help feeling an overwhelming sadness of *our* loss.

Once when I was giving such a glowing statement of how beautiful, wonderful, and superior this other plane of existence is, the person I was speaking to said "Then why do we stay here. Why don't we all just go over?" The reason why we don't just all leave and go over is because we were sent here for a purpose. This is a testing, a proving ground, an area for learning, and if we take things into our own hands and bring it to an unnatural end, it will all have to be done over again. Sieg has a beautiful saying he always uses whenever he is going through great turmoil: it is, "Await God's moment, which men call years. Do out the duty."

The indestructibility of the real "you" has been stressed previously. There is never a moment when you are not you! The very instant that the clock ticks out your last second here, it joyfully tocks in your first second there. Do you doubt this for a moment? Do you think that God, the giver of all life, would be content to be the God of dead things, for there are more dead than alive. Sheer reason tells us that He did not create the fantastic walking, talking, thinking miracle called man only to watch him go down to his end with the casket, brush His hands and say "Well, so much for that one!" The same source does not send out both life and death, no more than the same spring gives out both sweet and bitter water. Death leads but to resurrection, not resurrection *of* matter but resurrection *from* matter.

We do not belong to the earth any more than the child belongs to the school he attends during the day. When the end of our day comes, we rush home like the child to the bosom of our family, who gently enfold us and waft us away to ease the hurts and disappointments of our earth life and bid us rest before we are introduced to the glorious possibilities of our new existence.

Imagine the joy when the rest and the awakening have been accomplished, to find it was no dream: our loved ones are really there, and we are told that we may continue in our work if we so desire or do whatever else is of interest to us. That there is no limit to what or how much we can accomplish nor the quantity of help we can give to others, either to those there or to the ones we left back in the earth vibrations. The only sadness comes when we see the sorrow left behind, caused by those who mourn excessively and seem to have no faith in the greater reality.

It is not so much that we must think of this world as something to escape from but rather the other world as something to aspire to. As long as we are making one ounce of effort toward the upward climb, we are justified in feeling that the best is yet to come, just as the view becomes greater with every ascending step in climbing a hill. As the light of eternal hope beckons us ever onward, we go as our fathers before us have gone, hoping that the light we bear will have done its share to dispel the dark night of fear, so that our children who follow may be one step closer in their realization that there is a land of eternal day.

Epilogue

The labyrinthine workings of the subconscious mind, the mysteries of human and animal instinct, physical phenomena manifestly caused by no physical impulses, the vanishing of space and time in the supersensual activities of the mind, dominance of mind over matter—all these have been studied here and their implications have been pondered objectively and impassionately. The data and the reasonings based on them point to one and only one conclusion: There must exist a reality beyond the material reality of the senses. Call that reality what we may: heaven, the world of the spirit, a realm of high frequency vibrations of a force akin to electricity and light, we inhabitants of the twentieth century can no longer deny that it exists.

We accept on faith what scientists have discovered concerning the composition of matter. No man has ever seen an electron, but evidence points in the direction of its existence. It behooves us likewise to accept with an open mind evidence of the existence of that spirit world, to reject nothing, to reserve judgment until a large mass of data has been accumulated. But we must have patience, for investigation into that realm is slow because for some reason beyond our comprehension the phenomena coming from that world are sporadic and unpredictable, if not subject to downright whimsy. We must realize that in the long run there is no conflict between the two realities, between natural science and religion, for they are domains that command their own specific tools and their own methods. Our duty for the future of humanity and the progress of the universe is to push back with all our might and on *all* fronts the frontiers of the known into the mysterious domain of the unknown.

For there can be no dualism, there can be only one universe, since the mind can conceive of only one existence, manifold and complex as its manifestations may appear. For that reason our concept of a master mind, of a God, must be vast enough that He encompasses all the galaxies, discovered and undiscovered, and all time and space; must be wise enough to overcome and nullify within Himself and eventually within the universe all evil and all injustice; and must be minute enough to be all-pervading, down to the intricate design of the granular structure of a proton. We can no longer be satisfied with the war-loving avenging God of Israel, anthropomorphic in his need of sacrifice in return for mercy, but we must expand Him to the Divine Principle of justice that can tolerate no disharmony. Nor can we be content with Voltaire's watch-maker Supreme Being who has constructed a complex machine, wound it up, set the pendulum going and turned his back. The cosmic consciousness of the mystics has too clearly revealed God as the indwelling force, the divine spark within the human soul. "Ye are Gods," said Jesus Himself. Nor, finally, does the romantic concept of a Spinoza of an identity between God and the Universe satisfy us. A new definition of God, one that will synthesize all these aspects, one that will comprise Existence and Perfection in all their facets, must be found for modern man.

That is the challenge to today's leaders in philosophy and theology and to the researchers in the twilight zone between the here and the beyond. Today's youth is bewildered, is hungry, famished for answers thrown up by genicide, atomic warfare and probings into outer space on one hand, and, on the other, by tottering moral standards.

Our disorientation, our frustrations, all our strife and turmoil cannot be denied by a Pollyannaish optimism. We are beyond any shadow of doubt stuck in the most dangerous and the most climactic moral and material crisis since the dawn of humanity, with violence, death and the paralyzing fear of death staring at us on every side. On the other hand, we dare not forget one of the grandest of mottos the ancients have handed down to us: PER ASPERA AD ASTRA, "through asperity to the stars." The very story of life and evolution teaches us that lesson: That progress can be made only by victory over challenges. The tree that, sending its feeder roots into a tiny crevass, splits the rock to find new nourishment, humbly teaches us that lesson. The river that by the very constriction of its canyon walls develops sublime depth and power, grandly teaches us that lesson. Only by countering resistance from within or without can we develop our physical muscles, and likewise we can progress spiritually to the discovery of new truths in expanded consciousness only by developing our moral fortitude, taking adversity in stride and turning it to good. Only through effort can we ascend the heights. We will not be carried there by some kind "funicular" or destiny.

In reading the pages of these chapters, the attentive and sympathetic reader will have found his fear of death as the fear of final annihilation progressively weakening and perhaps falling off, as shackles fall off from the wrists of a freed prisoner. Death will have lost its sting and its black horror of oblivion, or worse, of everlasting torture, and will appear instead as a golden door leading to a brilliant world of new experiences and new spiritual growth and expansion. The yearning for that world of unbounded discovery, as it is described at the glorious end of the tone poem *Death and Transfiguration* by Richard Strauss—that yearning is the striving of Goethe's Faust. Yet even Faust, who has learned everything on earth there is to know, must work out his karmic development. He dare take no short-cut. Thus we, too, at whatever station in life we may find ourselves, from the lowliest to the noblest, from the poorest to the richest, we each have our task to perform, our duty to do out, our stream to forge, our mountain to climb. We may tear our hands on the rocks of opposition and be hurled into the crevasses of depression, yet at every turn we can pause to fill our lungs with the air of freedom and gaze back to the plains whence we have come. And onward and upward we go, in this life and the next, though the pinnacle be ever invisible, to ever greater perfection, from glory into glory.

Siegwalt O. Palleske, Ph.D.